Teacher's Guide
for **In the Shadow of Race:
Growing Up as a Multiethnic,
Multicultural, and "Multiracial"
American** by Teja Arboleda

Teacher's Guide
for **In the Shadow of Race: Growing Up as a Multiethnic, Multicultural, and "Multiracial" American** by Teja Arboleda

Christine Clark
University of Cincinnati

LAWRENCE ERLBAUM ASSOCIATES, PUBLISHERS
2000   Mahwah, New Jersey   London

The final camera copy for this work was prepared by the author, and therefore the publisher takes no responsibility for consistency or correctness of typographical style. However, this arrangement helps to make publication of this kind of scholarship possible.

Cover design by Kathryn Houghtaling Lacey

ISBN 0-8058-2873-7 (pbk.: alk. paper)

Lawrence Erlbaum Associates, Inc., Publishers
10 Industrial Avenue
Mahwah, NJ 07430

Books published by Lawrence Erlbaum Associates are printed on acid-free paper, and their bindings are chosen for strength and durability.

Printed in the United States of America
10 9 8 7 6 5 4 3 2 1

Contents

Contents

Preface

The purpose of this teacher's guide is twofold. First, it is to facilitate K–12, college, and university faculty in situating Arboleda's *In the Shadow of Race: Growing Up As a Multiethnic, Multicultural, and "Multiracial" American* (1998), within the fields of race relations and multicultural education and related disciplines. Second, it is to critique and problematize its content so that it can be used to stimulate critical thought, debate, and action oriented toward increasing social justice among its readers both inside and outside of the classroom.

Part I of the guide, Situating the Research in the Fields of Race Relations and Multicultural Education, does two things: First, it articulates Arboleda's contribution to the fields of race relations and multicultural education (chap. 1) and provides a context for understanding Arboleda's story within these fields (chaps. 2 and 3). In this latter regard, it has fewer specific references to *In the Shadow of Race* because here its primary function is one of outlining the major debates in the fields of race relations and multicultural education with respect to language, terms, and concepts (chap. 2) and issues of race and identity (chap. 3). Subsequently, Arboleda's story can be and is grounded in these debates. Second, it provides a critique of Arboleda's work and problematizes his voice (chap. 4).

Chapter 2, Language, Terms, and Concepts, explores how one's choice of language or terminology conveys one's consciousness in the discussion of related concepts. This chapter discusses specific terms (race, ethnicity, nationality, citizenship, culture, heritage, "American," "non-White," "minority," and People of Color, "Indian," "Hispanic" and "Spanish," African American, and "Oriental") and concepts (stereotyping vs. characterizing, prejudice vs. discrimination, assimilation vs. acculturation inclusive of the "American dream" and the "model minority," the politics of racial categorization, individualism vs. collectivism, biculturalism vs. multiculturalism, and cultural diversity vs. multiculturalism in the history of Turtle Island and the United States) that Arboleda references and the implications of various uses of them in the context of the political correctness debate.

Chapter 3, Race and Identity, connects Arboleda's struggle to four major topics most currently at issue with respect to dialogue on race: (a) race as a biological, social, and legal construction or reification; (b) racial identity development theory; (c) racial power dynamics; and (d) racial borderlands.

Chapter 4, Critique and Problematization of Voice in *In the Shadow of Race*, undertakes a rethinking of Arboleda's own perspective. It is important that readers not take Arboleda's perspectives (nor anyone else's, including those couched, even hidden, in the mundane so-called "objective" language plaguing most "traditional" textbooks) at face value. Rather readers should engage in analysis and questioning of all perspectives vis-à-vis their own.

Finally, PART II discusses the Implications of *In the Shadow of Race* for Multicultural Education (chap. 5), and Suggestions for How to Use *In the Shadow of Race* in the Multicultural Education, Race-Related Education, and General Studies Classroom (chap. 6), while PART III provides an extensive References and Additional Resources list.

As the author of this guide, while I have spoken from research in the fields of race relations and multicultural education, and in some cases, have drawn on the same from related disciplines, my own voice is manifest in my interpretation and rearticulation of this research, especially in PART I. In PART II and PART III, my voice is also present in that in offering up implications, making suggestions, and identifying resources, I draw from my own classroom experiences teaching race relations and multicultural education and in other subject areas over the last 20 years in K-12, college, and university classrooms. Clearly then, this guide represents my reading of Arboleda's story, and my voice, whether offered deliberately or inadvertently herein, as Arboleda's, should not be viewed as neutral or objective but likewise critiqued and problematized.

—Christine Clark

PART I

Situating the Research in the Fields of Race Relations
and
Multicultural Education

1

Introduction

ARBOLEDA'S CONTRIBUTIONS TO THE FIELD OF RACE RELATIONS AND MULTICULTURAL EDUCATION AND THEIR IMPORTANCE

Teja Arboleda's, *In the Shadow of Race: Growing Up as a Multiethnic, Multicultural, and "Multiracial" American* (1998), is a much needed contribution to the field of race relations and multicultural education in particular and many other fields in general (see Part II). The discussion of race in the United States has been, and to a large extent continues to be, framed in terms of Black and White. Framing the discussion in this way, instead of in terms of say shades of brown, encourages the dichotomizing of racial identity into only and either White or Black, ignoring the experiences of other People of Color(s) altogether. This has left Native American or American Indian, Latina and Latino, Asian, and "mixed" peoples with two choices: identify and attempt to assimilate with those in power, "act" White, or challenge power relations, "act" Black (Fordham, 1988; Haney López, 1996; Ogbu, 1986). In bringing this dynamic of racism to our conscious attention, Arboleda begs us to engage in the erosion of such linear and modernistically, either/or, constructed thinking (Giroux, 1977).

Even in the most progressively conceptualized race-related dialogues, there is, all too often, an underlying assumption that even if everyone is not in fact monoracial, everyone at least pays allegiance to or finds a home in only one race culture (Webster, 1992). Even dialogues in bilingual and bicultural education ultimately imply that although individuals may develop "bi" or even "multi" lingual and cultural "competency," they always favor one (Cruz, 1996). With Arboleda's example, and that of many "Others" like him, past, present, and future, especially those who comprise increasingly greater percentages of our student and general populations both domestically and internationally, these dialogues can be effectively challenged. These examples beg exploration of the questions: Where do "mixed" peoples fit? What is the role of the autobiographies of "mixed" peoples in our local and global society and, more specifically, in our classrooms? Must "mixed" peoples deny part of who they are in order to have other parts affirmed? Must "mixed" peoples choose a singular identity to accommodate the majority who live with the steadfast illusion that they are monocultural?

Understanding multiculturalism in a broad way, we come to understand that every individual has multiple cultural identities from which they operate each day: racial, ethnic, linguistic, socioeconomic, gender-related, religious or spiritual, sexuality-related, ability-related, generational, geographic, and so forth. Arboleda's example simply further multiplies the multiplicity of racial, ethnic, linguistic, and geographic origin in particular. In so doing, his contribution raises a number of other questions to explore: What is race? Ethnicity? Nationality? Citizenship? Culture? Heritage? Where does one of these descriptive parameters begin and another end? Who is a foreigner where? Can one be something by cultural socialization that they are not by heritage? Can one be something by heritage that they are not by cultural socialization? How does one define one's cultural identities? Can culture be communicated through biology? These and other questions are addressed in subsequent chapters of this guide.

But, Arboleda's contribution to the global dialogue on "cultural diversity" is not merely intellectual, philosophical, political, and/or academic, it is also affective. His story conveys the profoundly, pervasively, and persistently negative impact of racism on peoples' hearts, minds, and livelihoods (Bell, 1992).

We see this negative impact emerge in several recurrent themes in the text. Perhaps most devastating is the generationally recurring rage at the injustices racism brings to bear on a person, a family, a community, a people. Beginning with Arboleda's paternal grandmother and grandfather (chap. 2), then his mother and father (chaps. 5 & 6), then his brother and he (preface & chaps. 7 & 8), the legacy of such rage is passed down. The youngest generation, Arboleda and his brother, bear the burden of not simply the rage they have accumulated from their own experiences of racism, but also that which they have accumulated through vicarious associations with the experiences of their grandmother and grandfather, mother and father.

This rage leads these same family members toward a similar strategy to attempt to cope with it: the erroneous promise of geographic "escape;" the idea that somewhere things will be different if only that place can be found. In the absence of securing even a pseudo-utopia, even a mediocre one, in being unable to escape even a measure of the racism, they each in turn try in vain to escape themselves, their family, their history.

Arboleda's grandfather is born into Asian ancestry and culture in the Phillipines, but carries a Spanish surname due to the colonistic history of the islands. It is here that he was socialized to dislike Blacks. Through a political manipulation (see Haney López, 1996, see also the discussion in chap. 3 this guide) he "becomes" White, travels to the United States to become an "American," only to discover he is now perceived to be Black. Still disliking Blacks, he marries a woman of Native American, German, and African ancestry, who although culturally Black, has been socialized to "act" White, a so-called "privilege" afforded her by her light skin. The two relocate to the Phillipines where she tries to identify Filipina but is demeaned as Black. He then abandons her there with four children for 12 years (chap. 2).

Arboleda's father is born Filipino in the Phillipines where he lives for 12 years only to be abruptly relocated to the United States by a father he has never known. At some point he consciously discovers his mother is Black, is perceived Black himself, and yet subsequently sets out to proclaim himself as Filipino-Chinese. Through chance international correspondence, he finds a German-Danish (or so she thinks) woman who demonizes her light skin in favor of his dark skin while he does the opposite; clearly the makings of a Spike Lee sequel, "Jungle Fever II." He travels to Germany to meet her, eventually marrying her and getting her pregnant only to leave her there and return to the United States. She eventually joins him in the United States where they have a second child, both of whom they name as Filipino-German. The children are then sent to Germany without their parents where they learn their first language, German. After a few years, they rejoin their parents in the United States where they learn their second language, English. After a few more years, the whole family relocates to Japan, where the children learn their third language, Japanese (chap. 8).

As teenagers, Arboleda and his brother come to claim Japan as their home and Japanese culture as their own only to discover that as adult they will be forced to relocate to their "native" country . . . if only they knew where that was. Struggling in his career because of the stigma of being quintessentially "too ethnic," Arboleda experiments with his identity, first Italian, then Mexican. Finally, he makes a career for himself out of telling his life story, oddly, a career that requires constant travel (chap. 26). He has, in an understandably somewhat frenzied way, become so adept at instantaneously coping with culture shock, cross-cultural adaptation, that he coined his own expression, invented his own phrase, to describe the frenzied adeptness, "social integration overcompensation" (Arboleda, 1990). Social integration overcompensation describes Arboleda's experience of desire to belong, a desire so profound that in the effort he makes to realize it he goes too far, ending up more isolated than at the outset. There is always San Francisco, right? If he could just get someone there (or anywhere?) to give him a job based on his intellectual ability and not "in spite of" his physical attributes. The Reverend Dr. Martin Luther King, Jr.'s perhaps overquoted and often superficially invoked line, " . . . content of their character and not the color of their skin" (Public Broadcasting System, 1992) is, in this instance, most apropos. The simple retelling of Arboleda's story is exhausting. Imagine living it.

Arboleda's paternal grandmother and grandfather, his mother and father, his brother, and Arboleda himself, are all entrenched in the struggle to at once escape racism and find a "cultural home," the struggle to escape the pain of belonging essentially nowhere and perhaps everywhere simultaneously. They all run from parts of who they are at the same time that they quest to end their homesickness, still unable to find that "cultural home." In the end, Arboleda asks us to consider how the seemingly simple adage "Home Is Where the Heart Is" is perhaps quite complex and, in so being, more true for he and his family than anyone. And although there is resolution in this conclusion of his, there is the sense that it still resonates in at least a somewhat hollow fashion. His struggle continues (chap. 26).

2

Language, Terms, and Concepts

In this chapter, information is provided to facilitate educators in the situatation, critique, and problematization of Arboleda's language choices and the consciousnesses his choices convey throughout *In the Shadow of Race*, especially vis-à-vis the political correctness debate. Terms and concepts that Arboleda uses and/or that his discussion references, directly or tangentially, deliberately or inadvertantly, are explored in an effort to encouraging the grounding of his work within the sociopolitics of race relations and multicultural education.

LANGUAGE CHOICE AND CONSCIOUSNESS

The issue of language, word, terminology, or phrase choice is perhaps one of the most contentious in the general political climate sine the 1960s, and, more specifically, with respect to race relations and multicultural education (Nieto, 1996). The contentiousness of this issue correlates highly with the relation between linguistic characterizations of social membership groups (based on race, ethnicity, language, socioeconomic class, gender, sexuality, ability status, religious or spiritual affiliation, age and generation, size and appearance, geographic origin, and environmental concern among others) and the corresponding impact of these characterizations on group members' identity development (Giroux, 1996). Most important in this process is determining who is in control of these characterizations, who has the power to name. Clearly, members of traditionally underrepresented social membership groups (People of Color, people of every ethnicity other than Anglo Saxon, second language speakers of English, working-class people, women, Lesbian, Gay, Bisexual, and Transgender people, physically, developmentally, and emotionally differently abled people, people of every religion other than Christian, especially Protestant, people under 21 and over 65 years of age, people who are not reasonably thin or attractive, people from everywhere but the east coast of the United States, and environmentally concerned people among others) have been named by those with the most access to power at the institutional level in society (White, Anglo Saxon, native English-speaking, middle to upper class, heterosexual, able-bodied and at least theoretically able-minded and emotioned, Christian, usually Protestant, usually 21 to 65 year old, reasonably thin, reasonably attractive, east coast, environmentally indifferent or hostile men; Clark, 1993a). Divorced from the ability to name oneself, to characterize oneself, to in fact project one's identity, one becomes "fugitive" (Giroux, 1996; Macedo & Bartolomé, in press; Perea, 1995), one runs from imposed names and characterizations of one's identity that, all too often, demonize that identity by assigning negative qualities to it and/or by taking all positive association from it. For example, in a study done by Van Sertima (1992) of Egyptian civilization, it was determined that astronomy, art, mathematics, science, and technology were considered one body of knowledge. There was no suggestion that astronomy or art were less reliable measures or explanations of phenomenon than mathematics was. What was discovered, however, was that as art was separated out from science, so too were Egyptians separated from owning their scientific discoveries. Once art was relegated to a less important level, it was easier for subsequent civilizations to criticize it as an inaccurate representation of a particular previously existing civilization. Hence, Egyptians' images of themselves with very African features quickly turned more Mediterranean and eventually European as non-Egyptians and non-Africans began to (re)create those images. Once removed from controlling images of themselves, Egyptians also lost the credit for their discoveries as clearly the images of people now (re)connected with those scientific discoveries did not look at all African. Today, Blacks struggle to regain for their ancestors and hence themselves the recognition for a lot of what the Greeks are credited (Van Sertima, 1992).

The words we use convey a level of consciousness or lack thereof that, when applied to people in particular, are integrally connected to demonstrations of respect or disdain, respectively. The issue of language choice becomes most complicated when we consider that one person's conscious attempt to use language to convey respect can be received by another person as full of disdain. Such may reflect differences in consciousness or differences in experiences, different points of references. For example, one might choose to use the term *Black* to reference a person's racial membership group. One member of this group may reject this term in favor of the term *African American* which they may perceive to be more "contemporary" or to convey a more "liberatory" intent. Yet another member of this group may reject this term in favor of the term "*Negro*." In this latter example, the person is likely to be older and is associating the term Black with its usage to convey disdain in the early 1900s rather than with its usage to convey respect in the 1960s.

Given these and thousands of other parallel complexities, many people develop a sense of contempt that a good faith effort on their part may fuel the flames of discontent between groups. "Why bother?" is often the reply. Many argue that it is simply "too difficult" to figure out what is appropriate with whom, when, and so forth. Although there are no hard and fast rules, some basic guidelines to facilitate people in this endeavor may be useful. Multicultural education argues that it is generally best to:

1. Use the most contemporary or liberatory term or phrase to describe a group. For example, *Native American* or *American Indian* versus *"Indian;" Black* versus *"Negro"* or *"Colored;" Latina* and *Latino* versus *"Hispanic"* or *"Spanish;" Asian* versus *"Oriental;"* and *White* versus *"Caucasian;"*

2. Be more specific than less, using ethnic references rather than racial ones if you know this information. For example, *Navajo, Cherokee, Acoma* or *Nipmuck* versus *Native American* or *American Indian; Black American, African American, Ethiopian* or *Jamaican* versus *Black; Mexican, Mexican American, Chicana* and *Chicano,* or *Puerto Rican* versus *Latina* and *Latino; Japanese, Japanese American, Chinese,* or *Vietnamese* versus *Asian;* and *European American, Irish American, Irish,* or *French* versus *White;* and,

3. Ask someone what they prefer to be called or how they identify themself racially and/or ethnically than to assume (Nieto, 1996).

However, even in following these guidelines one can still end up conveying disdain when attempting to convey respect every time (Lipsitz, 1996). Some people will choose to identify themselves by what is generally considered a less contemporary or liberatory term or phrase or more general ones. This may be because they analyze the term or phrase differently and arrive at a more contemporary, a more liberatory conceptualization of them than is generally well-known. Or, this may be because they have not been challenged or have not accepted challenges to their own thinking about their identity. This latter instance is often characterized as "colonized" thinking, describing the insidious impact of colonization on colonized peoples' thinking such that, conditioned by the experience of colonization, they either do not even recognize it or they buy into it thinking that they will be rewarded for their allegiance to the colonizer (Freire, 1970).

Although the notion of colonization generally evokes references to a past historical era, it is important to point out that Puerto Rico is still, in the *most* formal sense, a colony of the United States. Yet, colonization need not be conceptualized in the formal historical and geographical sense. The process of colonization persists long after the physical colony is established. From a psychosocial perspective, the act of colonization continues to play itself out in the minds, hearts, and souls of both the perpetrator of colonization and its target (Fanon, 1967; Laing & Cooper, 1971; Sartre, 1976; Szasz, 1970). Having colonized, taken over, one's sense of importance relative to the colonized grows. Conversely, having been colonized, been taken over, one's sense of importance relative to the colonizer diminishes. This dynamic is then reinforced at the institutional level in society in terms of who has full access to participation in it and hence the power in it (the colonizer), and who has partial, compartmentalized, limited, or even no access to participation in it and hence no power (the colonized; Fanon, 1967; Laing & Cooper, 1971; Sartre, 1976; Szasz, 1970). Often, the colonized group or person attempts to win greater access to participation in the society by adopting the values and norms of the colonistic group or person; "If I think and act like they do, they will reward me for it." The contradiction here is that no matter how like the colonizer the colonized try to be, they are still and always will be constructed as more colonized, more "Other" than colonizer despite perhaps earning conditionally and only incrementally greater access to colonizer privilege in being identified as less "Other" than most "Others." In convincing the colonized group or person that they will be rewarded by playing rather than resisting, challenging, attempting to erode or eradicate "the game," the process of colonization continues indefinitely (Fanon, 1967; Laing & Cooper, 1971; Sartre, 1976; Szasz, 1970).

Although it is crucial that individuals and groups of individuals be able to name themselves, for this naming to have the empowering impact intended it must be undertaken in a context, created through political action directed toward the realization of social justice, in which there is at least an awareness of, a struggle against, if not complete freedom from mental colonization. Absent of this context, the whole process of self-naming is inauthentic, couched in the abyss of psychological control. Too, the political action necessary to bring this about must be likewise authentic, organic in nature, emerging from the colonized by the colonized for the colonized and directed toward their development and exercise of agency (Freire, 1970).

It is also important to remember that even when one asks someone, with the greatest respect, what they prefer to be called or how they identify themself, a person might may not only not welcome the inquiry as respectful, but may completely thwart it as contemptuous, enraging. Simply because one is attempting to develop a respectful consciousness about people different from oneself, one cannot expect to be immediately embraced by these different people. The true test of the genuineness of one's commitment to developing this consciousness lies in one's willingness to remain undeterred in developing it regardless of the reactions, be they positive, negative, or indifferent, by others. One's commitment evolves because one believes this is the right thing to do, not because it will get one something, win one influence or entrée; it is simply part and parcel of one's journey toward "becoming more fully human" (Freire, 1970).

POLITICAL CORRECTNESS

Understanding the complexities in the aforereferenced consciousness-raising process with regard to language choice even only superficially, many people dismiss it summarily as "unimportant," "not worth their time," an "imposition," and so forth. The misappropriation and manipulation of the phrase *political correctness* by the political right, their wielding of it as a clarion call to racism and other forms of discrimination, not only lends support to these dismissive actions but has the further effect of resanctioning colonistic thought and action (Bowen, 1993).

To understand the concept behind the phrase, political correctness, it is first necessary to locate this concept within the past paradigm, or dominant cultural ideology, out of which it emerged: modernism. It is also necessary to locate it relative to the current paradigm into which we have subsequently moved: postmodernism. The modernist paradigm suggests that humans are directed toward ascertaining absolute truth. Knowledge bases are broadened and pursued in earnest to either find for the first time or to defend what are believed to be long-standing essential truths (Dussell, 1993; McGowan, 1991; Rattansi, 1994; Smart, 1992; Young, 1990). Western society is still heavily entrenched in modernism, driven in the conquest to find concrete answers to aesthetic questions, guided by an either/or philosophy—either something is good or evil, right or wrong, black or white—and a cause and effect relationship—if one does this then that will happen (Dussell, 1993; McGowan, 1991; Rattansi, 1994; Smart, 1992; Young, 1990). The concept of political correctness was born out of this era; hence, the "correctness" part of the phrase. As result, it was initially postulated as a dogma, a benevolent dogma but a dogma nonetheless (Berman, 1992).

Postmodernism, like all "to be" or rather "already arrived" doctrines of thought, is much more complex than the incumbent modernism. It has replaced modernism by debunking it (Gould, 1996), revealing its insufficiency in accommodating cultural changes occurring in society, that is, its inability to offer adequate, much less plausible, explanations of these changes. *Modernism* generally only offered one explanation of anything; the "correct" one. Postmodernism suggests that truth is relative, not absolute, that something can be good and bad or neither, right and wrong or neither, white and black or gray, pink, purple, and so forth; at once both the union and integration of opposites (Dussell, 1993; McGowan, 1991; Rattansi, 1994; Rosaldo, 1993; Smart, 1992; Young, 1990). Many cultural critics believe that the advent of the postmodern paradigm was inevitable as society moved and continues to move to a hypertechnological state (LaClau, 1992; LaClau & Mouffe, 1990). Before technology, these critics argue, the "real" world existed along with truth and historical chronicity. Now, because of technology, reality is lost and with it truth and historical chronicity leaving us with antiabsolutism, antiessentialism, ahistoricity. For these critics, this signifies an end to history and the advent of what is now being called "New Times," a new historicism (LaClau, 1992; LaClau & Mouffe, 1990). Obviously, these critics are still grounded in modernism as this depiction of postmodernism's birth and the direction of its progression is a linear one, unicausal and unieffectual, absolute. A postmodernistically influenced cultural critic might assert that this depiction of postmodernism by the modernistically influenced critics is plausible, but so are many others. The real wisdom of postmodernism is that it teaches us to question all authority, even its own. Rather than debate *a* singular Truth with a capital "T," absolute or essential truth, postmodernism suggests that we debate plural truths with lower case "t's," antiabsolutist, antiessentialist truths (Dussell, 1993; McGowan, 1991; Rattansi, 1994; Rosaldo, 1993; Smart, 1992; Young, 1990). Furthermore, postmodernism suggests that we debate the questions of "benefit," that is, forget Truths, correctness, and so forth altogether, instead, look at who benefits from a particular point of entry into debate. Within postmodernism then, it is possible to articulate an ardent opinion, something that one wants to say or show the world about something, this is simply done from the perspective of relative benefit or truth, rather than absolute (Dussell, 1993; McGowan, 1991; Rattansi, 1994; Rosaldo, 1993; Smart, 1992; Young, 1990).

As Western society has been dragged, kicking and screaming, into the postmodern paradigm where most of the rest of the world has resided for some time, the concept of political correctness may now be postulated with much greater sophistication (Dussell, 1993; McGowan, 1991; Rattansi, 1994; Smart, 1992; Young, 1990). It is in this framework then, that the concept of political correctness will be discussed, understanding that aspects of it delineated, initially conceived of as absolute in the context of modernism, have now evolved into a point of entry into debate about it in the context of postmodernism (Dussell, 1993; McGowan, 1991; Rattansi, 1994; Smart, 1992; Young, 1990).

The phrase political correctness, and its derivatives, *politically correct*, and so forth, originated within progressive movements on the left in the United States during the 1960s (Bowen, 1993). In this context, the phrase was not used as a pejorative but as an acknowledgment that certain political positions adopted were, in fact, politically correct given the usually Marxian class analysis adhered to in arriving at these positions. That is, to say that one's position was politically correct implied that one understood, via the process of reading, researching, studying, thinking, and so forth, the class and other power dynamics involved in the process of forming a political agenda that was concerned with one's own place in society as well as others and was motivated toward the redistribution of wealth and power in society in an effort to effect real, as opposed to imagined, equity on the concrete, bread and butter, not theoretical, level (Bowen, 1993).

As the 1960s progressivish or leftish movements in the United States grew and people in them began reacting initially from their gut, as in the women's and Gay, Lesbian, bisexual and transgender movements (Nicholson, 1990; Warner, 1993), rather than a knowledge base acquired from reading, researching, studying thinking, and so forth, the phrase politically correct began to be used in a derisive fashion *within* the left by people who did not want to put forth the effort to read, research, study, think and particularly to coalition build, people who were only interested in furthering their own cause, like Gay White men (Warner, 1993). The phrase was also used by those who adopted politically correct politics without understanding the process of analysis involved at arriving at the positions embodied within them. This they did in an attempt to "look good" within left movements; but because of the superficial nature of their positions they needed to keep distance between themselves and those who might ask them to justify their positions in engaging in dialogue about various issues as is common practice in even casual conversation within the progressive left. To maintain that distance they might invoke the retort, "Oh, you're just trying to be 'p.c.,'" in response to a probing question for which they could not muster a coherent reply, in an effort to elude having their intellectual shallowness revealed (Bowen, 1993).

Most recently, the phrase politically correct has been discovered by the "old rascals of the so-called new right" (Bowen, 1993; Brenkman, 1995). And, this phrase is doing for them what the term *liberal* did for George Bush in the 1980s, it creates a context for dismissing large political constituencies by suggesting that it is not relevant to listen to, for example, Native Americans or American Indians who protest the appropriation of terms like Washington *"Redskins,"*

Cleveland *"Indians,"* Jeep *Cherokee,* and so forth for everything from sports franchises to cars (Bowen, 1993). When people want to address deeper issues of identity, when they want to engage in struggle to really understand one another, when they want to come together to address power dynamics and genuinely set forth a plan as to how to achieve cultural equity, the old rascals pull the phrase political correctness out of their repository of counterintelligence as though it were a clarion call to notions of whiteness, "reverse discrimination," cultural, intellectual, political, and economic dominance floating around in the recesses of collective unconscious of anyone and everyone in which they can instill a fear about the radical intent of those they describe in invoking the phrase (Bowen, 1993).

TERMS

Given Arboleda's focus, the discussion of terms herein will be limited to the general terms *race, ethnicity, nationality, citizenship, heritage, culture,* and to a few more specific terms and phrases related to these six, *"America," "non-White," "minority," People of Color, "Indian," "Hispanic," "Spanish,"* African American, and *"Oriental."* The discussion of the general terms and phrases: *language, socioeconomic class, gender, sexuality, ability statuses, religious* or *spiritual affiliation, age and generation, size and appearance, geographic origin,* and *environmental concern,* among others, and more specific terms and phrases related to these is also important. An exploration of such terms and phrases in the classroom might be an interesting way to extend the dialogues on language choice and consciousness beyond the scope of what Arboleda has begun, broadening the base of student multicultural awareness, knowledge, and understanding. Excellent supplementary resources for such adjunct discussion are *Teaching for Diversity and Social Justice: A Sourcebook* (Adams, Bell, & Griffin, 1997), *Stick, Stones, & Stereotypes* (Marshall, 1991), and *Camp Lavender Hill* (Shepard & Magnaye, 1998).

In beginning the discussion of the aforereferenced terms, as well as the subsequent discussion that will be undertaken of related concepts, it is important to acknowledge that any such discussion can have the effect of tending to define the objects of discussion. Perhaps eventuating definitions is inevitable, however, it is important to remember that terms and concepts, especially those attempting to describe human realities in a sociopolitical context, are constantly changing, evolving, and so forth, and so should not be conceptualized in a static fashion. The ensuing discussion should be viewed as suggestive, not prescriptive, to encourage further, different, and new suggestion and not, in any way, to reify the ever elusive terms and concepts at issue. Analysis deriving from the ensuing discussion should be oriented in a delimiting rather than limiting fashion.

Race

Race is perhaps one of the most complicated terms to discuss in all of human language (Cashmore, 1996). In chapter 3 of this guide, we explore the etiology of the concepts behind the term itself. For now, let us consider race as a term socially constructed to generally describe categories of people based on the perception (albeit incorrect as the discussion in chapter 3 of this guide elucidates) of physiological differences, the most overriding of which is skin color and relatively recent geographic origin (since the break-up of Gondwanaland[1] as is discussed in greater detail in chapter 3 of this guide; Dott & Batten, 1981). Today, five different racial groups are generally refered to (Gillan, 1992):

1. Native Americans or American Indians—people geographically indigenous to the Americas (North, Central, and South);

2. Blacks—people geographically indigenous to Africa;

3. Asians—people geographically indigenous to Asia;

4. Whites—people geographically indigenous to Europe; and,

5. Latinas and Latinos—people also geographically indigenous to the Americas (North, Central, and South), generally held to be of mixed Native American or American Indian, African, and European ancestry.

Given these groupings, Middle Eastern peoples, Arabs and Jews in particular, are considered to be racially White despite having group members with skin colors ranging from very light to very dark and despite the proximity of their indigenous geographic origin to Africa (Gillan, 1992). Obviously, wide variances in skin color exist in all five of the groups mentioned. And, indigenous origin is highly dependent on what time frame in human history one is referencing. These are two of the many reasons that the term race is so problematic; what it attempts to define does not exist (Gillan, 1992). Arboleda's ancestry brings this reality into stark relief.

Ethnicity

Ethnicity is a term generally used to describe subgroups within a race based again on geography, but generally even more recent, contemporary, geographic origin (Cashmore, 1996). Ethnicity also carries with it the innuendo of cultural traditions, values, norms, and so forth associated with each subgroup (Jackson, 1976b). Within the Native American or American Indian race, ethnicities might include Ute, Lakota, Aztec, Taina and Taino; within the Black race, ethnicities might include Haitian, Egyptian, Ghanaian, and Barbadosan; within the Latina and Latino race, ethnicities might include Costa Rican, Nicaraguan, Venezuelan, and Colombian; within the Asian race, ethnicities might include Filipina and Filipino, Hmong, Tibetan, and South Asian (from India); and within the White race, ethnicities might include Czechoslovakian, Italian, Palestinian, and Iranian. In giving these examples it should already be apparent why the term ethnicity is problematic in terms of what it attempts to approximate (Ang, 1995; Gay, 1985; Hall, 1991a, 1991b, 1996; San Juan, 1991).

Nationality and Citizenship

Given the preceding examples of ethnicity, how are they distinguishable from country of origin, *nationality*, and/or *citizenship*? (Balibar, 1996). For some people, all four of these things might be the same; for other people they may all be different, in which case how are they independently discernible? For example, someone could be ethnically Jamaican, born in Jamaica, with Jamaican citizenship. Someone else might be ethnically Jamaican, from Jamaica, living in the United States, but a French citizen. In this latter case, are they a French or U.S. "national," of French or U.S. nationality? Are nationality and citizenship synonymous? If not, how are they predictably distinguishable from each other? If yes, then why is it that some people make differentiations between them? (Balibar, 1996).

Heritage and *Culture*

To add insult to injury here, let us throw the terms *heritage* and *culture* into the mix. Heritage may be most simply defined in terms of one's ethnic bloodlines. Culture is more difficult to define. Culture may be thought of as a system of meaning making; however an individual or group of individuals make meaning and use that meaning to interact with the world (Jackson, 1976b); "How one is raised to view and perceive life" (Smith, 1991). Hence, culture can be individually specific or group specific depending on the scope of the evolution of the system of meaning making, the view and perception of life (Gates, 1996; Geertz, 1973; Hall, 1992). Arboleda asks the question, can someone be something by culture that they are not by heritage and vice versa? With respect to Arboleda himself, can he be culturally Japanese if he is not Japanese by ethnic bloodline? Conversely, is Arboleda culturally Filipino if he was not raised in the culture, socialized to its system(s) of meaning making, its view(s) and perception(s) of life?

Going back to the examples just given, if someone is born in the United States to Jamaican born and culturally socialized parents, but adopted by a Black American family, both by heritage and culture, who subsequently moves to France, is this person ethnically Jamaican? Jamaican only by heritage? Culturally Jamaican, Black American, or French? A U.S. citizen and national or a U.S. citizen with French nationality?

To further complicate things, many times religious affiliation is also often thrown into the ethnicity equation. For many people, being Jewish or Muslim in particular, describes simply their religion (Bulkin, 1984; Jackson, 1976b; Kantrowitz, 1996). For others, however, it describes both their religion and ethnicity, carrying with it that innuendo of cultural traditions, values, and norms (Jackson, 1976b). For others still, those who do not practice the religion into which they were born say, it describes simply their ethnicity (Jackson, 1976b). For example, nonpracticing but Jewish-born persons may consider themselves only ethnically Jewish, and many Muslims from Serbia and Croatia consider themselves ethnic but not religious Muslims. This can extend to other religions as well. Nonpracticing but Christian-born persons, who, just to complicate things further, are say practicing atheists or agnostics, or even converts to another religion, may still consider themselves ethnically Protestant or Catholic.

Clearly, the concept of culture is integrally connected to many social membership group delineations—ethnic culture, language culture, gender culture, Lesbian culture, Deaf culture, generational culture, geographic culture, and so forth—which hold within them the innuendo of cultural traditions, values, and norms, systems of meaning making, ways of viewing and perceiving life indicative of each group. For example, although ethnic culture is superficially associated with food, clothing, music, and holidays (Nieto, 1996), it is far more profound, far-reaching, and complex, extending to many aspects of life such as codes for the appropriate expression of respect and etiquette, and may shape what is considered funny, beautiful, and so on. Profundity, far-reaching nature, and complexity are characteristics indicative of every type of culture, whether based on social group membership or some other criterion (on professions such as law enforcement, higher education, art, or based on social interest (cop, academic, "artsy," or sorority, fraternity, or other club culture), and so forth; Nieto, 1996).

America

Arboleda uses the term *American* to describe people from the United States. The use of this term to describe only these people speaks to the arrogance of U.S. citizens in appropriating a term referencing an entire geographic region for themselves alone (Haney López, 1996). Canadians and Mexicans are, like U.S. citizens, *North* Americans. Hondurans and Argentineans are also Americans, Central and South Americans, respectively. The arrogance here is magnified by Whites in the United States who often take the appropriation of the term American even further, using it to reference only light skinned, blonde haired, blue eyed U.S. citizens. Arboleda's experience of being told to go back to wherever he came from (preface and chaps. 12, 14, & 20) is a perfect example of this. Someone who looks like Arboleda is not an American, based on "common knowledge" of what an American is supposed to look like (Haney López, 1996). The common practice of asking long-standing, multigenerational, U.S. citizens, who do not fit the "common knowledge" notion, where they are from originally compounds this arrogance further. At once, it perpetuates the myth, the White lie so to speak (though not little—as if White lies ever really are), that Whites in the United States are not originally from somewhere else themselves (i.e., Europe) and that, for example, Mexicans are (the border crossed them not the other way around, which should be obvious given state names like Colorado and Florida, and city names like San Diego and Santa Fe; Donato, 1997).

Perhaps exacerbating the practice of this arrogance is the clumsiness of trying to take our nation name and apply it to our people. Whereas the transition from Canada to Canadian is smooth, that from United States to United Stateser is awkward at best (Nieto, 1996). In developing a consciousness of this arrogance, we can compensate for it by remembering all of *America*, as in the Americas, by remembering that Whites in the United States do in fact have an adjective to describe what kind of American they are, as in European American, and by broadening our "common knowledge" conceptualization of what a North American, a U.S. citizen, and America really are to include not just light skin, blonde hair, and blue eyes, but dark skin, black hair, and brown eyes, and everything in between.

"Non-White," "Minority," and *People of Color*

Arboleda also uses the term *"non-White"* to collectively reference Native Americans or American Indians, Blacks, Asians, and Latinas and Latinos. His use of this term is problematized beyond what is undertaken here in chapter 4 of this guide. The more contemporary, liberatory, term is *People of Color*, but as with all language choices, this term does not go uncontested, it is not universally accepted (Jackson, 1976). The term People of Color emerged in reaction to the terms "non-White" and *"minority."* The intent of all of three of these is, as already stated, to collectively reference Native Americans or American Indians, Blacks, Asians, and Latinas and Latinos. The term People of Color attempts to counter the condescension implied in the other two: "non-White" describes people in terms of what they are not, in the negative, instead of in terms of what they are, in the affirmative, and "minority" describes people as minor, less than, relative to major, more than, not simply in the numerical sense (which will soon be in fact reversed) but in the aesthetic sense as well, less than as in less human.

Ironically, although People of Color is considered a contemporary, liberatory term, the same term is found in meeting minutes of the city council (or facsimile thereof) in Worcester, Massachusetts dating back to the late 1800s (Worcester Historical Museum Archives, see Part III). Also, given generationally different reference points as discussed earlier, many older, especially Black people receive this term as synonymous with the term *"colored,"* generally considered to be derogatory (again, the perception of even this term as derogatory or not is generationally based, some older Black people, and White people of virtually any age socialized in overtly racist households or communities, may consider "colored" a term of respect used in lieu of *"nigger"* or other dehumanizing epithets).

Although it would be impossible to review every term used to describe a social membership group, there are a few terms that warrant this review because despite their being politically problematic group references, they remain a part of common usage in the everyday.

"Indian"

One such term is *"Indian,"* used to describe Native Americans or American Indians. This term was coined for this group of people by Columbus (Rethinking Schools, 1992). This is an example of a colonizer imposing a name on their colonized as previously discussed. But furthermore, Columbus chose this name for the people he "met" in the Americas because he thought he was, geographically speaking, in what Europeans at that time named the "Indies." Both the colonistic context and navigational error aspect of this term have encouraged its rejection (Rethinking Schools, 1992). However, many Native American or American Indian people have chosen to continue to use the term "Indian" (hence the interchange of the term *Native American* with the term *American Indian* throughout this guide), more often in the context of American Indian but even alone because it is so much a part of even their language that it is hard to give up (Rethinking Schools, 1992). In some ways, its negative historical etiology has been acknowledged and dismissed and the term has been, in essence "reclaimed" from this etiology as if divorced from it, as if it no longer pays attention to it, as if it no longer knows this history.

It should be noted that the practice of reclaiming terms, concepts, symbols, and so forth from colonistic and otherwise derogatory inceptions and/or appropriations is controversial. Some people feel that doing such is a positive and liberatory practice that has the effect of making impotent the derogatory aspect by replacing it with a positive one, by taking the negative power in it away from the wielder in taking or retaking the term, concept, symbol over and reconstructing it positively. In addition to Native Americans or American Indians, many other social membership communities have engaged in this practice. For example, the Lesbian and Gay community's reclamation of the straight community's derogatory use of the term *"Queer"* as a term of both affection and political affirmation, taking the negative power out of the term used as an epitaph by heralding it positively, even to the point of naming a Lesbian and Gay activist group "Queer Nation" (Warner, 1993)

Other people feel that any attempt at reclaiming is futile and suggest that the practice is rooted in subconscious or unconscious self-hatred. This camp asks the question, Why would one ever want to embrace a term conceived for so hateful a purpose? (Bengis, 1987; Clark, 1999).

"Hispanic" and *"Spanish"*

Two other terms that warrant review are *"Hispanic"* and *"Spanish,"* both terms used interchangeably with Latina and Latino. "Hispanic" is a U.S. census term, another example of a colonizer imposing a name on their colonized (McLaren, 1995). Furthermore, this term has been dissected into "His Spain" referencing the previous colonizer and the paternalism and patriarchy inherent in the act of colonization. The word "Hispanic" is thought to be an Anglicization of the Spanish word, Hispana and Hispano, meaning literally, Spanish, once again referencing Spain, the major colonizer of what are now referred to as Latin American countries. Many people (including Latinas and Latinos themselves, usually those still caught in the web of colonized thinking) choose to characterize Latinas and Latinos as singularly of Spanish descent, ignoring the Native American or American Indian and African components of their ancestry (Giroux, 1996). As previously alluded to and as is discussed in greater detail in chapter 3 of this guide, this is another example of a people's culture being made "fugitive," something from which they flee. Why would one want to claim Native American or America Indian, or, worse, African ancestry when one could claim Spanish instead? (Giroux, 1996). This is but one more example of allegiance to the colonizer ideology of White blood, European heritage, lightness as positive, Black blood, African heritage, darkness as negative.

The U.S. Census Bureau also coined the terms *"Black Hispanic"* and *"White Hispanic."* However, when asked to clarify what these terms mean exactly, senior managers, staffing offices in 25 major metropolitan areas, could not give a coherent definition of either (Jenkins, 1994). The impression is that Latinas and Latinos are essentially being asked to choose either a Black or White identity; once again, race is dichotomized into either Black or White (Rattansi, 1994).

To complicate things further here, it is important to consider the ways in which meanings of terms and phrases may change when they are translated into other languages. This is because whereas these terms and phrases may be more or less literally synonymous, their meanings are socially constructed differently by the members of the various cultural communities who employ them as we just saw in the discussion of the terms Hispanic and Hispana and Hispano.

To begin with, in Spanish, words ending in "a" are said to be feminine and those ending in "o" are said to be masculine. In other so-called "romance" languages like Italian, French, Portuguese, and to some extent, Greek, this is also the case; the word endings that indicate femininity or masculinity are simply different. Even in English, words have feminine or masculine roots but, divorced from our Latin linguistic roots, we do not often recognize word gender. Because gender is recognized in Spanish and many other languages, aspects of its use are sexist. One way that this sexism is manifest is in the convention of referring to a mixed female and male group with words that employ the masculine ending, for example, referring to all people, women and men, from Latin America[2] as Latinos instead of Latinas and Latinos (Nieto, 1996). The feminine ending is used only when the group described includes solely women. To challenge this linguistic sexism, and despite it being somewhat cumbersome, it is best to use both endings when the group referred to is mixed. In the spirit of a sort of a linguistic affirmative action, using the feminine ending first is encouraged (Lam & Pruyn, 1998). Although gender is often not recognized in English, it, too, is unequivocally sexist. For example, in English, there is the convention (parallel to that described for Spanish) of referring to all people, women and men as "man" or "mankind," or that of using only the male pronoun when speaking about an individual of undetermined gender, as in the sentence, "If the student is learning, *he* will be able to demonstrate . . . " (Loveday, 1982). To compensate for this in English, and again, despite it being a bit awkward, it is best to use human or humankind in lieu of man or mankind and to use both male and female pronouns or a gender neutral pronoun when speaking about an individual of undetermined gender, as in the sentence, "If the student is learning, she or he (or s/he or they) will be able to demonstrate . . . " It is better to bear the wrath of grammar teachers than to perpetuate discrimination in continuing to use sexist language.

Another cross-linguistic complexity can be found with respect to the term Black. We have already seen how complicated understanding this term as a racial group reference can be simply in one language, English. Translating it into, say for example, Spanish further complicates its understanding in this regard. In

Spanish, the term Black can be translated as, among other things, Negra and Negro, Morena and Moreno, and Prieta and Prieto. Depending on what Spanish-speaking community one is in, these terms can convey Black in a positive or negative manner, highly correlated with skin color or without reference to it at all, as well as in a purely descriptive fashion, that is, without a positive or negative connotation. For example, in some Puerto Rican communities, negra or negro, which means literally the color black, can be used to describe an object as black, negra or negro, as in English, to describe a dark skinned person as Black, Negra or Negro, also as in English, but also, unparalleled in English, to endear a person of *any* skin color. In this latter case, often a diminutive suffix is added to magnify the endearment as in Negrita or Negrito, which translate roughly as little Black or dark one. Pedro Pietri, a noted Puerto Rican poet, finishes his famous poem, "The Puerto Rican Obituary," with the line, "Aqui to be called negrito [o negrita] means to be called LOVE" (Pietri, 1989). However, despite this endearing social construction of blackness, darkness, one has to wonder if underlying it is not some latent infantile innuendo directed at dark skinned people; as if what is being conveyed is a connection between blackness, darkness, and cuteness, and somehow having the effect of stripping especially adult Black people of their maturity, forever relegating them to the diminished stature implied in the innuendo of cuteness (Gould, 1996).

An endless number of other cross-linguistic comparisons (including comparisons with "non-oral" or sign languages) could be offered as examples here. There is no finite way to undertake an analysis of such comparisons. Hence, such analysis will have to emerge and develop in concert with the consciousness and cross-linguistic knowledge base of those involved in it.

African American

The term *African American* has been more recently problematized, causing many people to return to the term Black or to use the term *Black American* instead. There is some indication that the term *African* derives from the name *Africus* or *Africanus* who is thought to have been of European ancestry and an early colonizer of the continent now bearing a facsimile of his name, Africa. This is another example of a colonizer imposing a name on their colonized (Van Sertima, 1992).

"Oriental"

"*Oriental*" is a term unfortunately still used interchangeably with, perhaps even more frequently than, *Asian*, which is the more contemporary and liberatory term chosen by Asians to describe themselves. "Oriental" carries with it a geographic bias perhaps greater than all of the other terms and phrases heretofore discussed, because in colonistic fashion it refers not just to the people of one country or geographic region but to an entire hemisphere, its people, its history, everything about it; it is a name that the West has imposed on the East, and hence by which it negatively characterizes it in its totality (Said, 1985). In a word, it conveys everything negative that often many different epithets are required to get across; Asians as "exotic," "sexual," "stoic," "passive," "inscrutable," and so forth. At its worst, it can be argued, "Oriental" is equal in derogatory intent vis-à-vis Asians as "nigger" is vis-à-vis Blacks (Said, 1985).

Clearly, language choice and consciousness vis-à-vis race relations and multicultural education are phenomenally complex. But, in their complexity lies endless possibility for dialogue oriented toward improved, or at least improving, cross-cultural, broadly conceptualized, understanding.

CONCEPTS

A review and discussion of a few concepts will also facilitate discussion on *In the Shadow of Race*. Some of these concepts can be most easily discussed as juxtapositions of each other: stereotyping versus characterizing; prejudice versus discrimination; and assimilation versus acculturation.

Stereotyping Versus Characterizing

Stereotyping can be understood as the practice of assigning a generally negative attribute of one person in a group to everyone in that group. Characterizing may be understood as the practice of describing a group by generally positive attributes, often but not always common to its members. The important differences between these two concepts are twofold. Stereotyping is generally negative[3] and suggests that something is always true about a group, whereas characterizing is generally positive (attempting to describe the shared qualities of a group that approximate their culture) and suggests that something is generally but not always true about a group. In characterizing, one considers what is generally the case for the group but always keeps open the possibility that for any particular individual from that group what is generally the case for the group is, in fact, never the case for the individual; this entails a complex balancing act (Jackson, 1976b).

Prejudice Versus Discrimination

Prejudice can be understood as a usually negative prejudgment about someone or something that occurs at the level of thought (Allport, 1958; Nieto, 1996). Discrimination can be understood as the carrying of a prejudice into action (Nieto, 1996). It is important to remember that we must engage in prejudgement every day for survival. For example, it is necessary to be able to prejudge the rate of speed at which a car is traveling down a street we need to cross in order to determine if we have enough time to get to the other side without being hit. Prejudice only becomes problematic when it is applied to human situations. And although everyone is prejudiced with regard to human situations, everyone can still work to become less so by developing meaningful relationships with people from groups with respect to which they hold prejudices such that we interrupt those prejudices, replacing them with real experiences, before we carry those prejudices into action (Jackson, 1976b).

Assimilation Versus Acculturation

Assimilation can be understood as the inadvertent loss or deliberate abandonment of one's own social group membership identity for or in favor of that of another (Jackson, 1976b). It can occur passively (inadvertent loss) or actively (deliberate abandonment). Acculturation can be understood as the acquired and rehearsed ability to interact in accordance with the social membership group norms of one or more groups of which one is not a member (Jackson, 1976b). Acculturation can also occur passively (inadvertently) or actively (deliberately). Acculturation is akin to developing cross-cultural or multicultural interaction competency, the ability to move from one's own culture (particularly in terms of practicing the norms associated with it) to another (again, particularly in terms of practicing the norms associated with it) or, more generally, to move between cultures. Arboleda's "social integration overcompensation" (as discussed in chap. 1 of this guide) is, in essence, a hybrid of assimilation and acculturation; acculturation gone too far that ends up having the long-term effect of assimilation (Arboleda, 1990, 1998).

The American Dream

In the United States, members of many immigrant groups (both voluntary and involuntary; Nieto, 1996) as well as members of many geographically indigenous ethnic groups, actively undertake the process of assimilation in search of the so-called American dream. As previously mentioned, there is the belief, or perhaps the hope, that if one behaves as those in power do that one will be correspondingly rewarded. The quintessential reward held out to those-who-would-assimilate is the promise of realizing the American dream—a utopian middle-class life. Of course, especially in the context of capitalism, even if everyone played the assimilation game perfectly, the promise of the American dream would remain largely elusive for most as capitalism necessitates that someone be on the bottom for others to be on top. The more there are on top, the exponentially more are needed on the bottom to support the weight (Marx, 1904).

The "Model Minority"

The term "model minority" is also associated with assimilation and the American dream. It conveys the notion as referenced previously, that most "minorities" or People of Color are not "model," that is, not like the majority, White people, the de facto model against which they are measured. But, it also conveys the notion that if an individual "minority" person or Person of Color is willing to become "model," an "exception to the rule," by assimilating, they will be rewarded with the American dream. Certain racial groups have been held up as "model minorities" against which other "minorities" are then measured. In particular Asians (as previously footnoted), and among Asians specifically Japanese and South Asians (from India), are socially constructed as "model minorities" (Lee, 1996). Ironically, part of their so-called "modelness" is based on the perception of them as "passive" in contrast with the perception of particularly Blacks as "rebellious." This is ironic because the perceptions of passivity and rebellion are, more often than not, a cross-cultural misreading by Whites who assume silence in Asians is an expression of passivity and vocalness in Blacks an expression of rebellion when these behaviors usually mean neither in either culture (Mun Wah, 1994). Furthermore, the perceived vocalness of say the Irish and the perceived passiveness of say the Navajo, did not preclude the Irish from securing the so-called rewards of assimilation to beyond simply White, but further Anglo Saxon Protestant norms and the American dream (Alba, 1990; Ignatiev, 1995; Jester, 1992), nor facilitate the Navajo in achieving "model minority" status, respectively. Hence, not only are the "model minority" status donners fickle in their donning, but they never don status-enough to provide complete, entire, full access to participation in democracy. That is, no matter how well a "model minority" assimilates, or even plays the game via well-honed acculturation, they will never beat the game designers at their own game (Delgado, 1995).

Politics of Racial Categorization

In chapters 21, 22, and 24, Arboleda challenges the U.S. census to do away with racial categorization altogether, but settles, in the short-run, for the addition of a multiracial category to the census choices. His challenge raises the question, Why do we need to keep track? The reason, it would seem, is to make sure Whites maintain the majority through the manipulation of immigration policy just at the moment it looks as if the so-called "minorities" will become at least the numerical "majority" (Haney López, 1996). There is no way of knowing the answer to this question for sure, but questionable undertones haunt it whatever the undertones are as is discussed further in chapter 3 of this guide.

The addition of a multiracial category raises two other difficult questions. First, if people have the opportunity to choose the multiracial category instead of being forced to align with a single racial one, what will be the ensuing impact on the "Of Color" single race category members who rely on their numbers for political voice? (Jenkins, 1994). Second, how will enforcement of affirmative action and equal opportunity legislation be carried out? That is, will people who identify themselves as multiracial be considered protected class members? If so, how will the legislation be amended to include them without providing Whites who feign multiracial heritage the opportunity to erode the effectiveness of the support protected class status provides by claiming it for themselves under their multiracial auspice? (Johnson, 1995; Rose, 1992). If not, will anyone currently aligned with a protected class racial group choose to forgo this protection and use the multiracial category? (Jenkins, 1994). The answers to these questions can not be predicted. Only time will provide the answers. But, they do raise provocative and important issues for reflection and debate in the classroom.

Individualism Versus Collectivism

Within the debate regarding issues of cultural identity is the position espoused mostly by Whites that the ultimate goal should be for everyone to abandon their racial, ethnic, and other group memberships in favor of simply being "American." The notion that what is American is not racially, ethnically, and otherwise culturally entrenched (White, Anglo Saxon, English-speaking, Protestant, and so forth) is largely an uncontested one (Allen, 1994; Apple, 1997; Bonnett, 1996; Clark, 1999; Clark & O'Donnell, 1999b; Delgado & Stephancic, 1997; Frankenberg, 1993b; Hardiman, 1979, 1982; Helms, 1990a, 1995; Keating, 1995; Lipsitz, 1995; Nakayama & Krizek, 1995; Novick, 1995; Powell, 1996; Roediger, 1991; Shohat & Stam; 1994, Stowe, 1996; Young, 1979). But, most White people fail to realize that their freedom to be and comfort in being "ruggedly individual," as Arboleda characterizes it in chapters 14 through 18, is a function of American culture being in fact their culture (the hidden or not so hidden, depending on one's perspective, Eurocentric culture). In being White, English-speaking, and at least middle-class, the ability to function seemingly independent of the support of a cultural community, to move with relative freedom in society, is a forgone conclusion (Allen, 1994; Apple, 1997; Bonnett, 1996; Clark, 1999; Clark & O'Donnell, 1999b; Delgado & Stephancic, 1997; Frankenberg, 1993b; Hardiman, 1979, 1982; Helms, 1990a, 1995; Keating, 1995; Lipsitz, 1995; Nakayama & Krizek, 1995; Novick, 1995; Powell, 1996; Roediger, 1991; Shohat & Stam; 1994, Stowe, 1996; Young, 1979). People of Color, second language speakers of English or non-English speakers, and members of the working class and working poor, know the reality of the limitations within which they live, which limit their freedom and require their interdependence with a like cultural (racial, linguistic, and/or socioeconomic) community (Delgado, 1995). What Whites, native English-speakers, and at least middle-class people fail to realize is that the delimitation on their freedom also requires their interdependence with a like cultural (racial, linguistic, and/or socioeconomic) community. Because White people do not experience themselves as racial or ethnic, they do not experience others like them in that way either and hence do not perceive their association with like others to be based on cultural affinity. By encouraging all Americans to abandon all other cultural affiliation, Whites are, in reality, creating another double standard for People of Color. Unable to recognize their own cultural affiliation outside being American or rather, that being American is in fact their cultural affiliation (White, English-speaking, middle-class), they are also unable to recognize that in asking People of Color to become simply American that they are asking them to do what they would never do themselves. This has the effect of only further disadvantaging People of Color and advantaging Whites although it is erroneously couched in the rhetoric of uniting us all (Allen, 1994; Apple, 1997; Bonnett, 1996; Clark, 1999; Clark & O'Donnell, 1999b; Delgado & Stephancic,

1997; Frankenberg, 1993b; Hardiman, 1979, 1982; Helms, 1990a, 1995; Keating, 1995; Lipsitz, 1995; Nakayama & Krizek, 1995; Novick, 1995; Powell, 1996; Roediger, 1991; Shohat & Stam; 1994, Stowe, 1996; Young, 1979).

Biculturalism Versus Multiculturalism and Cultural Diversity Versus Multiculturalism in the History of Turtle Island and the United States

The United States has always been culturally diverse. Even before we came to know the geographic area now referred to as the United States as such, when Native Americans or American Indians were the only peoples inhabiting the North American continent (which the Haudenasaunee[4] named, "Turtle Island"), there was ethnic, linguistic, gender, sexuality, spiritual, ability, generational, and geographic among other forms of cultural diversity (Anzaldua, 1987; Brown, 1971; Dean & Suchman, 1964; Gresson, 1996; Ignatiev, 1995; Loewen, 1995; Omi & Winant, 1994; Takaki, 1993; Van Sertima, 1976, 1992; Williams, 1970; Zinn, 1970, 1980). As other racial and ethnic groups also came to inhabit the island/continent, this diversity only broadened. But diversity means simply difference, it does not in any way describe the context in which those differences exist. Multiculturalism may be understood to in fact reference a positive context for differences to exist in: "the process of recognizing, respecting, and valuing cultures other than one's own, stressing an appreciation for the impact of difference across race, ethnicity, language, socioeconomic class, gender, sexuality, ability status, religious or spiritual affiliation, age and generation, size and appearance, geographic origin, and environmental concern" (Smith, 1991, p. 4). So, to reiterate, although the United States has always been culturally diverse, the context in which that diversity has existed has ranged from indifferent to hostile, but it has never been affirming (Anzaldua, 1987; Brown, 1971; Dean & Suchman, 1964; Gresson, 1996; Ignatiev, 1995; Loewen, 1995; Omi & Winant, 1994; Takaki, 1993; Van Sertima, 1976, 1992; Williams, 1970; Zinn, 1970, 1980). Multiculturalism as a concept for contextualizing the cultural diversity in the United States is still very new. Although we may be superficially familiar with its process (as delineated previously), we are largely inept at proactively engaging in it. This becomes our greatest task, to figure out how we can come together, affirmed and valued in all our uniqueness, willing to face and work through the persistent ugly hostilities between us, so that we may finally practice radical democratic citizenship (McLaren, 1997).

NOTES

[1]The once combined land mass of what is now called South America, Africa, India, Australia, and Antarctica (Dott & Batten, 1981).

[2]Brazil's location in South America and Belize's location in Central America make both countries part of Latin America. But, their histories of colonization by the Portugese and the British, respectively, rather than the Spanish, make referencing Brazilians and Belizeans as Latinasand Latinos complicated. Culturally, Brazilians

and Belizeans are in some ways as "Latina and Latino" as Uruguayans, El Salavadorans, and so forth, and in other ways they are radically different, as radically different as Uruguayans are from El Salvadorans, and so on. This is just another example of how complicated so-called racial (based on skin color and geographic origin) and associated cultural identities are.

[3]Even when a stereotype is intended to be positive as with the common stereotype, "Asians are good at math," it has negative impact; as an Asian whether or not you are in fact good at math, you are locked into the expectation of performing well in it. This dynamic is discussed in greater detail in this chapter under the heading, The "Model Minority."

[4]This is thought to be the original name of the Native American or American Indian nation more commonly referred to as the "Iroquois." As has been discussed with respect to other peoples throughout this guide, the name "Iroquois" is thought to be a name imposed on the Haudenasaunee by the Europeans and, furthermore, to have negative connotations as "devious," "traitorous," and "evil" (Zinn, 1980).

3

Race and Identity

In this chapter, information is provided to facilitate educators in the situatation, critique, and problematization of Arboleda's conceptualizations of race and racial identity expressed throughout *In the Shadow of Race*, especially with respect to the debates on: (a) the social, biological, and legal construction and reification[1] of race, (b) racial identity development theory, (c) racial power dynamics, and, (d) racial borderlands pedagogy. Conceptualizations that Arboleda articulates and/or that his discussion references, directly or tangentially, deliberately or inadvertantly, are explored in an effort to encourage the grounding of his work within the sociopolitics of race relations and multicultural education.

RACE AS A SOCIAL, BIOLOGICAL, AND LEGAL CONSTRUCTION AND REIFICATION

Social Construction and Reification of Race

Because the concept of *race* is sociopolitically constructed (Ignatiev & Garvey, 1996; Webster, 1992), to reference it perpetuates its reification, to refrain from referencing it obscures the persistent, pervasive, and seemingly permanent reality of racism (Bell, 1992; Nieto, 1996). This is the quintessential contradiction with which Arboleda leaves us. In exploring how race came to be reified, how it came to be a socially constructed entity, we will also come to see how even Arboleda's most well-intentioned plea, first to expose this, and then to destroy the concept of race in its entirety, if realized, may actually exacerbate racism and other forms of discrimination instead of eroding them.

To begin this very complicated discussion, it is necessary to return to the discussion of truth and postmodernism introduced in chapter 2 of this guide. In the context of postmodernism, Truth, in the absolute sense, is itself revealed as a social construct (Dussell, 1993; Geertz, 1973; McGowan, 1991; Rattansi, 1994; Rosaldo, 1993; Smart, 1992; Young, 1990). A common example of this, one often pointed to in the field of multicultural education, is that history is written by those in power (Loewen, 1995; Takaki, 1993). So while a subscriber to modernism might purport that Columbus "discovered" America, a postmodernist might argue that he also "invaded" Turtle Island. Which statement is, in fact, true, or rather, the absolute Truth? In the context of postmodernism, the context in which Arboleda's experience is affirmed rather than denied or pathologized, the answer depends on your point of entry into debate (Clark, 1993a).

Absolute truth is what we agree it to be; if the floor tile has a color and five people see it and agree that the color of that tile is green then the absolute truth is that the tile is green. But, if a sixth person comes on the scene and says that the floor tile is blue, what then becomes of the absolute truth of the tile's color? In that moment, truth is no longer absolute, it is relative. To reestablish the absolute truth, the five might suggest that the sixth person is "color blind," meaning that the way this sixth person sees color is not as they, the *majority*, see it, therefore there must be something wrong with the sixth person's perception, but not, of course, their own. In this way, the experience of the sixth person is denied and pathologized in an effort to maintain the absolute nature of the truth, an absolute truth that has now not only been constructed but reifed, taken from its aesthetic context and made concrete. If the sixth person persists in asserting a dissenting opinion, the absolute truth, if only for another moment, is once again made relative. The five might retaliate by asking this sixth person to remove her or himself from the premises where the tile is; out of sight out of mind. In this person's absence, absoluteness is restored to the truth. But then the five sit down to watch the news and low and behold, there the sixth person is, in front of the premises where the tile is with a picket sign asserting, before an array of television cameras, that the tile is blue! Now what? What if the sixth person gathers support from others who might agree that the tile is blue, what then? So the five launch a counter-protest to discredit the sixth, they try to label the sixth "immoral," "criminal," even "crazy," in an effort to further deny and pathologize the sixth person's experience and recommend control over truth in the absolute sense. But this backfires and the sixth gains supporters. Finally, the five decide that the only way to make sure that the truth can be made to stay absolute is if they silence, kill, any opposing voice. And so they do, they hire an assassin (who by the way agrees that the tile is green if there is a decent paycheck involved) and the assassin takes out the sixth and all the sixth's supporters. Absolute truth reigns supreme once again, unsoiled by the wild rantings of any would-be dissenters. Anyone who might have thought the tile was blue has either changed their opinion or is keeping their mouth shut for fear that the assassin will come for them if they were ever to let their perspective be known.

Clearly, in place of floor tile color one could insert police brutality, immigration, abortion, the legalization of same sex marriage, and so forth. The five could all be White or all male or all heterosexual or all able-bodied . . . and the sixth could be Black or female or Gay or have a disability. The scenarios that now come to mind given the theoretical parameters offered in the floor tile example, begin to look quite familiar and a whole lot less theoretical (Delgado, 1995).

In so deconstructing absolute truth, it is now possible to see it as the illusion that it is, that it has always been (Dussell, 1993; McGowan, 1991; Rattansi, 1994; Rosaldo, 1993; Smart, 1992; Young, 1990). Furthermore, it is also now possible to see how broad the brush and how thick the paint with which the illusion has been painted. To continue the analogy here, multicultural education serves as a form of paint thinner; as the paint is thinned more and more, Arboleda's face, experience, and truth is brought, increasingly, into greater resolution.

In chapter 11, Arboleda reveals an example of how race was socially constructed for him. This example is quite poignant: he goes to the library, and, in a book that he later discovers is a "picture bible," sees pictures of naked "White" people (people from the Middle East depicted as light skinned and with European features, save the one or two wise men, portrayed as subservient, and Judas, the traitor, who were portrayed with dark skin). His reaction to the nudity, even as a child, is one of embarrassment. Juxtaposed with the retelling of this incident, Arboleda then reflects on the reaction he had to seeing pictures of naked Black people in *National Geographic* or in UNICEF commercials on television and realizes that these pictures did not embarrass him because it seemed natural to him that Black people would be naked. So, as a first grader, Arboleda had already internalized socially constructed aspects of the concept of race. Arboleda suggests here that Blacks, as portrayed on the pages of *National Geographic* and in UNICEF commercials, are more "sexual," "primitive," "savage" than Whites and in these roles nudity befits them, it is "natural." Conversely, Whites who the media, school textbooks, and so forth portray as sexually discreet, technologically advanced, and "civilized," are, in these roles, demeaned by nudity, provoking of embarrassment (Ehrlich, 1994; Media Educational Foundation, 1995). Haizlip (1994) has pointed out that given the images of Black people in publications like *National Geographic* and in television commercials like those for UNICEF in which a starving Black child, belly distended, dirty and covered with flies is the focus, Blackness becomes demonized to such an extent that it is no wonder Black people are made fugitive from themselves (Giroux, 1996), run from who they are by buying fade creams to lighten their skin and chemicals to straighten their hair; with images of Blackness like those depicted in the media, why would anyone want to identify themselves as Black?

Arboleda also brings up the issue of cross-racial adoption vis-à-vis identity development (chap. 26). Arboleda's treatment of this issue is problematized in chapter 4 of this guide but in the context of the current discussion it is interesting to consider how identity is revealed so starkly as a social construction in the circumstance of cross-racial adoption. Black children raised by White families have coined themselves "biologically Black," in an effort to describe how culturally not Black, in fact how culturally White they feel they are (Haizlip, 1994). Going one step further, even children adopted into families where race per se is not an issue still struggle with ethnic identity. In one instance, a White child adopted by a White family who knew nothing about the child's birth family except for the first name that family chose for the child, came home from school with the assignment to research her family history by interviewing grandparents about their immigrant experience, particularly, their experience of coming through Ellis Island. The magnitude of Eurocentric ethnocentrism underlying this assignment is phenomenal. What if a child in this classroom had no grandparents or no access to grandparents because of death, divorce, and experience of domestic or sexual violence? What if a child in this classroom was Native American or American Indian, a people with no "immigrant experience" to speak of? What if a child in this classroom was Black and her or his grandparents' so-called immigrant experience was involuntary and via an auction block, not Ellis Island? What if a child in the classroom was from California and their grandparents immigrated through a different port of entry to the United States? For the adopted White child at particular issue in this classroom, this assignment opened up questions regarding ethnic identity. The adoptive mother offered the child the opportunity to claim the ethnic identity and immigrant experience of the adoptive family or to try and discern another, perhaps more accurate one. Toward the latter end, the mother and child researched the etiology of the child's first name, imagining that it may have had some familial significance to the birth parents. They discovered its ethnic roots and the child constructed an ethnic identity and immigrant story based on a sort of composite immigrant history of the ethnic group in an effort to complete the assignment. The adoptive mother and the child even planned to take a trip to the chosen country of origin. On discovering the extremely cold climate in this country, the mother sarcastically lamented that she had not suggested to her child to claim Puerto Rican ethnicity to make for a more climatically welcoming trip (Haizlip, 1994).

With examples like these and especially Arboleda's, it is hard to imagine how anyone ever came to accept truth, race, ethnicity, culture, and so forth as anything other than a social construct. How then can we understand the process by which race became reified? (Cruz, 1996). Ironically, it seems that racism, or at least prejudice and discrimination based on physical characteristics, not only preceded the social construction and reification of race itself, but created the context for it to subsequently emerge.

It should be noted at the outset of this discussion that assessment of inferiority or superiority, any assessment of value, can be arrived at via ways of knowing seemingly completely antithetical to so-called science, research, factual evidence, and so forth (Dussell, 1993; McGowan, 1991; Rattansi, 1994; Rosaldo, 1993; Smart, 1992; Young, 1990). These are in themselves socially constructed and culturally entrenched concpets (Dussell, 1993; McGowan, 1991; Rattansi, 1994; Rosaldo, 1993; Smart, 1992; Young, 1990). Cosmology[2] is perhaps a more holistic way of knowing (Dussell, 1993; McGowan, 1991; Rattansi, 1994; Rosaldo, 1993; Smart, 1992; Young, 1990). An interesting example of cosmology compared with Western science as ways of knowing can be found in the example of a specific geographic spot in South America. The spot was long known to medicine people as having great healing power. Western scientists dismissed it until Western medical doctors visiting the area witnessed positive changes in patients who had been to the spot. Their curiosity piqued, Western scientists flocked to the spot to find out what might account for the health improvements and discovered that the spot was highly magnetic. Suddenly, Western scientists "confirmed" the healing power of the spot. But, if the medicine people already knew of the healing power of the spot then Western scientists only confirmed via another way of knowing what was already known (LaClau, 1992; Lipsitz,1995, 1996; Macedo, 1994; Perea, 1995). Applying this to ways of knowing about superiority and inferiority, many people who have grown up in racially, ethnically, culturally, and so forth diverse communities in which they have had positive and meaningful relationships with people different from themselves, do not need Western scientists, anthropologists, the law or any other formal discipline that attempts to confirm or disconfirm Eurocentrically imposed notions of racial superiority or inferiority. Rather, they know from their lived experience, cosmologically, that superiority and inferiority are a false measure of human worth regardless of race (Delgado, 1995; Gould, 1996; Haney López, 1996; hooks, 1993; Loewen, 1995; Takaki, 1993; Zinn, 1970, 1980). In the abstract sense, the worth of all human beings is the same, differences in worth attributed to race, ethnicity, culture, income, education, and so forth are politically constructed theory (like "science" and "law") as the ensuing discussion elucidates (Delgado, 1995; Gould, 1996; Haney López, 1996; Omi & Winant, 1994). In the concrete sense, an individual's worth may best be based in how reliable and sincere (also socially constructed measures) a person they are. It is in this spirit that the following discussion should be contextualized.

Biological Construction and Reification of Race

In *The Mismeasure of Man* (1981) by Stephen Jay Gould, the history of prejudice and discrimination based on race, ethnicity, geography, socioeconomic class, and gender are reviewed, vehemently interrogated, and seemingly exhaustively debunked. What Gould does in this book is to examine every claim of biologically determined inferiority and superiority and the so-called scientific methods employed to support such claims. In his examination he discovers arguments that identify four so-called "inferior classes" of humans that, in order of supposed increasing inferiority are: non-Western European men, the poor, women, and People of Color. Underlying this argument is the contention that within each inferior class, the evolutionary process that produced its members was stunted, prevented from reaching the highest possible human evolutionary outcome (by producing a White, Western European, upper-class man) because the genetic information required to reach this outcome was not a part of the genetic pool at conception. One by one, Gould reviewed not only the arguments to this effect but the so-called scientific methods, research, and experimentation on which the arguments are supposedly based. And one by one, by reviewing actual lab notes, actual hypothesis, reproducing actual experiments, and so forth, he was able to reveal the myth of biological inferiority. He exposes contradictory results recorded in lab notes, he uncovers mathematical incongruencies and fallacies in research hypotheses, and he makes obvious the inability of the experiments engaged in to prove the desired result.

Despite the utter thoroughness and integrity of Gould's review, the notion of the biological inferiority of people in the four so-called inferior classes remains reified. In so being, it is accepted by what is likely the majority of U.S. citizens, if not consciously then at least subconsciously, as the absolute truth. It is facilitated by overtly racist works like *The Bell Curve* (Hernstein & Murray, 1994), which Arboleda appropriately mocks in the preface. Unfortunately, to add insult to injury, the United States exports White American, Western Eurocentric racism to the rest of the world both via such works and the mass media in general that Arboleda confronted everywhere he traveled, especially in Japan in the White mannequins, the posters of White women, the airing and reairing of *Baywatch,* and so forth that he believed ultimately contributed to Asian self-hatred, in particular, their desire to destroy their Asian features and replace them with European ones (chaps. 11 & 12).

What Gould's book does not do however, is to question why the scientists who attempted to prove biological inferiority and superiority based on certain social group memberships not only set out to do this but did so with such resolve that despite the fact that their research repeatedly disproved their hypothesis they would rather forge their research results than admit the contrary, the reality. In examining their motives, we must return to the historical context in which they lived. Western Europeans voraciously engaged in territorial conquest under the auspices of "manifest destiny," supposedly the bringing of civilization to the uncivilized in the name of "God" (Loewen, 1995; Miller, 1996; Takaki, 1993; Zinn, 1970, 1980). If the masses of Western Europeans thought that Africans and Native Americans or American Indians were their biological and hence intellectual and "moral" equals, it is unlikely that they would have been so easily able to condone what was so obviously the ruthless and violent rape and pillage of these peoples, the women and children in particular, their homes, communities, and life resources (Loewen, 1995; Miller, 1996; Takaki, 1993; Zinn, 1970, 1980). By socially constructing the object of colonization as "less than," the tyranny waged against this object could be easily rationalized as being "for its own good," "to its betterment," and then dismissed as nothing more than an act of "taming," as in the "breaking" of a "wild animal," the making of a "savage" people, a biologically, and hence intellectually and "morally," inferior (but conveniently "physically superior") class of people "civilized" (Loewen, 1995; Miller, 1996; Takaki, 1993; Zinn, 1970, 1980).

The evolution of thought regarding human etiology is complex. An examination of so-called "legends of creation" from around the world are remarkably consistent, leading anthropologists to believe, as Kunjufu (1995) also stated, that an event occurred but was understood and hence described in a variety of ways in different cultural communities (Gillan, 1992). The convergence in the descriptions is accounted for by the presumption that the event at issue in each description was, in fact, the same event, its description was simply filtered through different cultural lenses (Dussell, 1993; McGowan, 1991; Rattansi, 1994; Rosaldo, 1993; Smart, 1992; Young, 1990). For example, the legend of creation in the Christian bible contends that at least the first man was created by God, and the first woman from the man's rib. Some Native Americans or American Indians believe that people "sprang from the ground like trees," emerged, like all other living things, from the earth. Western anthropologists argue that humans evolved from apes (Clark, 1993a). All perspectives on this historical eventuality are valid and should be affirmed in the classroom as part of the relative truth that will, perhaps someday, bring us all closer to the whole truth. For purposes of discussion here, the Western anthropological perspective warrants further attention.

Early Western anthropologists, functioning in a modernist context, argued that human evolution from apes occurred via what has been called the "three root theory" (Gillan, 1992). This theory suggests that simultaneously in the geographical areas now known as the continents of Africa, Asia, and Europe, in a slow linear developmental fashion, apes gave way to early humans (Gillan, 1992). Subsequent Western anthropological arguments emerging in the context of postmodernism, argue that the kind of evolutionary event that caused the emergence of humans from apes is so extraordinary that for it to occur in one part of the globe would be phenomenal, for the same event to occur not only in three parts of the globe but to do so simultaneously would be, in a word, fantastic (Gillan, 1992). This perspective is based on the perception that rather than slowly, linearly, and developmentally, the evolution from ape to human was perhaps more like a leap, an instance of "punctuated equilibrium," a largely unexplainable jump in the biology of a species or from one species to another. This argument has been associated with what is called the "three root theory" and is more widely accepted in contemporary anthropology today (Gillan, 1992). The single root theory suggests that all humans emerged from what is now called Africa, hence its characterization as the "cradle of civilization" (Gillan, 1992).

Various theories regarding why we ended up looking so different from one another emerged subsequently (Gillan, 1992). The consensus seems to suggest that as humans migrated from a common geographical home (before, during, and after the break-up of Gondwanaland, the once combined land mass of what is now called South America, Africa, India, Australia, and Antarctica; Dott & Batten, 1981), they were exposed to different climatic conditions. It is thought that again, either over a long period of time or in the fashion of punctuated equilibrium, physiological changes in people's make-up followed, making their survival in different climates easier (Gillan, 1992). For example, in very hot climates, people grew tall and thin to allow heat to better radiate, and their skin darkened to protect them from overexposure to the ultraviolet rays from the sun; in very windy climates, people grew shorter and more round and their eyelids enlarged, attributes that protected their bodies from being blown away and their eyes from dirt and sand; people in very cold climates grew more body and facial a hair to keep them warm and their skin lightened to afford them the opportunity to absorb as much of the very distant sun's vitamins as possible. Today, it is argued that we are all still evolving, ever-refining our physiologic adaptation to our climatic conditions (Gillan, 1992). However, with the advent of technology, many of us are now able to switch from one climate to another with great ease (hopping onto an airplane, a train, or into a car), not to mention that most of us spend a great deal of our time in temperature controlled settings. These developments are thought to be having the effect of slowing down our continued adaptive evolution. The fact that today in any one geographical location in the United States we may all look very different is not a function of biological superiority or inferiority, but rather biological perfection: To survive, all of our ancestors had to become perfectly adapted for the climate in which they lived and each one of us has inherited different pieces of that perfection (Gillan, 1992).

Initially, Western anthropologists in both the single and three root theory camps argued that three distinct races of people could be identified based on categories of physiological characteristics: skin color, facial features, and torso proportions (Gillan, 1992). These races were named "negroid," "mongoloid," and "caucasoid," roughly equivalent to what we now call Black, Asian, and White (note the racist construction of the referencing of Down's syndrome children as having "mongoloid" features; Gillan, 1992). Problems arose as Western anthropologists tried to predictably identify and categorize the skin colors, facial features, and torso proportions which distinguished one race from another (Gillan, 1992; Gould, 1996). First, in all three groups the same three chemicals responsible for producing skin pigmentation were found in varying proportions: melanin, a brownish chemical; carotene, an orangish chemical (what makes carrots orange); and keratin, a clearish chemical. Because the proportion of each chemical found in the systems of members of the same group was found to vary more widely than in those of members of different groups, skin color could not be used as a reliable determinant of racial group membership. That is, differences in the variance in skin color between people within a race was found to be greater than between people across different races. When Western anthropologists looked at facial features and torso proportions, the same results ensued. Without a regularly predictable criterion or set of criteria on which to predicate categorization, the notion of race as concrete, tangible, has been largely debunked among most anthropologists (Gillan, 1992; Gould, 1996).

As mentioned briefly in chapter 2, it is thought that Native Americans or American Indians are of Asian desent, believed to have migrated across the Bering Straight and into the Americas (Gillan, 1992; Loewen, 1995; Takaki, 1993). Latinas and Latinos are thought to be the combination of Native American or Asian, African, and European descent, emerging as a result of these three groups' coming together in the Americas just prior to, during, and just after the time of European colonization (Gillan, 1992; Loewen, 1995; Takaki, 1993). The "just prior to" reference is based on an emerging body of research suggesting an African presence in the Americas before the arrival of Europeans (Time Table of African American History, 1997; Van Sertima, 1976, 1992). Previously, it had been argued that the African presence was simultaneous to the European one (arriving with Europeans as navigators, e.g. Pedro Alonzo Niño; Time Table of African American History, 1997) or later as "slaves" (Van Sertima, 1976, 1992).

Today, Western anthropologists suggest that based on patterns of social mixing and hence procreation, Latinas and Latinos were but the first of what may now be over 2000 commonly reproduced racial combinations of peoples (Gillan, 1992; Takaki, 1993). For example, in El Paso, Texas it is common for Mexicans, Mexican Americans, or Chicanas and Chicanos and White Americans of varying ethnicity to mix: in Miami, Florida it is common for Cubanas and Cubanos or Cuban Americans and/or White Americans of varied ethnicity and/or Haitians or Haitian Americans to mix; in Los Angeles, California it is common for Black Americans and Chicanas and Chicanos to mix; and in San Francisco,

California it is common for Asians or Asian Americans of varied ethnicity and White Americans of varied ethnicity to mix, and so forth. Although many hope, including Arboleda (chaps. 21, 22, & 24), that this mixing will eventuate the end of racism, that future generations will be so mixed no one will be able to even surmise a specific racial group membership, the greater likelihood is that discrimination will simply be based on skin color alone, instead of skin color along with the presumption of racial, ethnic, or cultural group membership, heritage or nationality (Delgado, 1995; Haney López, 1996; Omi & Winant, 1994).

Legal Construction and Reification of Race

The persistence of discrimination in this manner can be attributed to another social construction of race, not biological, but legal. In *White by Law: The Legal Construction of Race* (1996), Ian Haney López recounts that as Western anthropological arguments reifying race and biological ones reifying superiority and inferiority were debunked and began to erode, legal ones emerged in their place, reinforcing the reification of race and the notion that White people were superior, and, therefore, deserving of at least greater if not exclusive access to participation in democracy in the United States. Referencing us back to Arboleda's innuendo as to why do we keep track of how many people there are of each race, we now discover what has been perhaps the reason all along, as alluded to previously, the preservation of the White numerical and political status quo.

According to Haney López (1996), during the period following the Emancipation Proclamation of 1865, theoretically ending legalized slavery, through to the 1950s in the United States, a little known immigration requirement was developed and enforced that required immigrants to the United States to prove that they were either "of African ancestry" or "White." And the language here is crucial, not "Black" or "of European ancestry," not "Black" or "White," and not "of African ancestry" or "of European ancestry." Although proving ancestry is a fairly concrete endeavor (though not always easily accomplished as, for example, neither birth nor death records on many Native Americans or American Indians and Black Americans were even kept prior to the early 1900s), proving that one is a color is certainly not. How does one argue in a court of law that one is White, especially if one is Asian, given that this legislation was oriented primarily at preventing Asian immigration to the United States? Haney López cites a number of cases of mostly Asian would-be U.S. immigrants. Only a very small number of the cases were ever granted a day in court, the rest summarily dismissed based on the plaintiff's "obvious inability" to successfully prove African ancestry or that they were White. It should be noted, that of the cases cited, in none did the plaintiff try to argue that they were of African ancestry. Perhaps this was because such was perceived to be harder to prove but perhaps this was because no one in their right mind would try and immigrate to the United States under the auspices of being of African descent during Jim Crow segregation (Haney López, 1996).

In a particularly landmark case cited, an Asian plaintiff had a White Western anthropologist expert witness make a scientifically compelling biologically based argument whereas his lawyer made an equally compelling political one, as to why the plaintiff was White, only to have the judge rule against them all (Haney López, 1996). The judge argued that although the plaintiff may be White anthropologically, biologically, and/or socioculturally, he did not "look" like what "common knowledge" tells "Americans" a "White" person "looks" like, and therefore he would not be allowed to immigrate. So much for Western science! The premise that used to be the cornerstone in determining absolute truth in favor of racism now broadened in such a way as to challenge racism has become the "baby being thrown out with the bath water." In its place is "the rule of common knowledge" (Haney López, 1996). The social construction of absolute truth begets the biological construction of it begets the legal construction of it; that floor tile is green damn it, and it is going to stay green.[3]

A relatively new branch of jurisprudence has emerged in an effort to challenge the notion that the law is a blunt instrument, unbiased and neutral; that any imperfection in it is a function of the players within the legal system, the prejudices that they, as individuals, bring to the interpretation and application of the law, the enforcement of the system. This branch of jurisprudence is called "critical legal studies" (CLS) and, applied to the issue of race exclusively, "critical race theory" (CRT; Bell, 1992, 1995; Cruz, 1996; Delgado, 1995; Delgado & Stefancic, 1997; Flagg, 1993; Guiner, 1994). Essentially, what CLS and CRT theorists do is apply critical theory to the law with specific regard to issues of race. What they argue is that the law itself is not a blunt instrument, but that it has been deliberately socially constructed (from its inception) and reconstructed (everyday) with the biases of those in power (generally upper-class White men) inherent in it, thus it is biased against "Others." Examples of this bias are amazingly simple to find. For instance, in the 1950s the Racketeering Influence and Corrupt Organizations (RICO) statutes were enacted specifically targeting Italian Americans stereotyped as organized crime members (Jenkins, 1994; Miller, 1996). In the late 1980s and into the 1990s, the RICO statutes were expanded into what are now referred to as Gang laws, specifically targeting Latino and Black male teenagers stereotyped as gang members (Jenkins, 1994; Miller, 1996). And yet, since the so-called founding fathers conceptualized the Constitution, no such statutes or laws have ever been developed to specifically target Whites and White collar criminals, corporate organized crime, corporate gang members (Jenkins, 1994; Miller, 1996). If written and then applied without bias, the RICO statutes and Gang laws would both find the founding fathers to be repeat offenders (Franklin, 1966; Jenkins, 1994; Miller, 1996; O'Brien, 1996).

At the same time that criminal law has become more race conscious and hence biased, civil law is becoming more race neutral and hence also biased, succumbing to the cries of "reverse discrimination" by namely White men; White men faced with merely the suggestion that "Others" should have legal assistance in trying to break into what continues to be the White Male Club begun by the so-called founding fathers (what is, in essence the Ku Klux Klan with sheets removed donning instead three-piece suits; Jenkins, 1994; Miller,

1996). The notion that Affirmative Action and Equal Opportunity legislation is discriminatory toward White men is in no way based in reality as 96% or more of all senior executive level and 80% or more of all middle management level positions in government, business and industry, health and human services and education are still held by White men who compose only about 30% of the general population (Delgado; 1995; Jenkins, 1994; Miller, 1996).

What CLS and CRT theorists argue is that when "Others," especially People of Color, learn to play the legal game to their advantage, the rules of the game are suspended or changed to maintain the status quo (Bell, 1992, 1995; Cruz, 1996; Delgado, 1995; Delgado & Stefancic, 1997; Flagg, 1993; Guiner, 1994). And this has been the case, not just with respect to the "rule of common knowledge" in immigration cases, but throughout history (Haney López, 1996). An historical example of this lies in the experience of Native Americans or America Indians vis-à-vis the U.S. government with respect to land treaties. Five nations (most notable the Cherokee nation) who became known as the "five civilized tribes," learned to negotiate the U.S. legal system in an effort to make legally enforceable land treaties in accordance with the oppressors' rules, using these rules for their own benefit, or at least protection. In absolutely every case, the U.S. government summarily broke the treaty and no court in the nation raised an eyebrow over it (Delgado; 1995; Lazarus, 1991). A more contemporary example exists in the O. J. Simpson case. Despite what people feel about the verdict, O. J. Simpson is one of the few Black people in the country with enough money to hire a high priced attorney. His attorney, Johnny Cocharan, is one of the few Black attorneys (among the many likewise highly skilled ones) who has been able to gain access to such a high profile legal arena in order to play the game on behalf of a Black client (Miller, 1996). Together they played the game extremely well with a mostly Black jury and won; the first time in our nation's history that a Black person accused of a capital crime against only White people was acquitted (The Education vs. Incarceration Clearinghouse, 1998; Miller, 1996). And they won only to hear cries that the legal system was in need of reform as a result (Miller, 1996). Why weren't these cries heard when the White police officers who beat Rodney King, a Black man, were acquitted with the help of a skilled White attorney and a mostly White jury? (Miller, 1996).

More recently, CLS and CRT theorists have begun to focus on differences in how People of Color and Whites are viewed in the criminal justice system (Bell, 1992, 1995; Cruz, 1996; Delgado, 1995; Delgado & Stefancic, 1997; Flagg, 1993; Guiner, 1994). For example, the death penalty is 4.3 times more likely to given to a defendant if their victim was White rather than Of Color. This speaks volumes about relative values placed on life based on social group membership (Jenkins, 1994; Miller, 1996).

In an interesting short story, noted critical legal theorist, Derrick Bell (1995), showed how the U.S. legal system can be manipulated by those in power at a moment's notice. In his example, Black people are sold back into slavery to racist Whites from another planet in exchange for fossil fuel and elaborate environmental purification systems that will extend life on earth. This, he argues

could, in fact, be done in the name of national security and nothing in the law,
nor any act of protest could prevent it.

Challenging the Construction and Reification of Race

In the preface, Arboleda struggles to affirm and reaffirm himself as a "liberal,"
that is, open-minded, accepting of differences, forward-thinking. What Bell, CRT
and CLS tell both Arboleda and the rest of us is that liberal is not only naive, it
preserves the status quo (Hardisty, 1996). To truly change the social, biological,
and legal construction, production, and reproduction of race and racism, we must
be utterly radical in our approach; we have to critically analyze the way in which
the system is vehemently self-preserving and find new ways to effect change
(Bell, Gaventa, & Peters, 1990; Bigelow, 1990). Being open-minded, accepting
of differences, and forward-thinking is like taking a stroll in a mine field, you
could have a really pleasant time or you cold get blown to pieces. Instead, we
must prepare for the worst and expect the best, commit ourselves to bringing
about social justice through radical democratic citizenship, through getting
involved, staying involved, taking a stand, and following it through to a positive
end, an end that ultimately opens up greater access to participation in democracy
for all (Adams, Bell, & Griffin, 1997; Bell, Gaventa, & Peters, 1990).

Just such a radical approach toward truly challenging the construction of race
and racism is postulated by a relatively new journal called *Race Traitor* (Ignatiev
& Garvey, 1996). The journal's motto is, "Treason to Whiteness is Loyalty to
Humanity." The journal argues that to end racism, whiteness as a sociopolitical
construct must be abolished, even as it pertains to the White antiracist struggle.
This is because White antiracists (much like racists) become so invested in their
status as such that they reify both race and whiteness, simply perpetuating not
dismantling racism and White privilege. That is, White antiracists are taught to
confront injustice but not if it causes them to lose White race privilege. This
argument could be expanded to the circumstances of almost any other form of
discrimination, for example, the notion of a gender traitor or treason to maleness
being loyalty to humanity (McIntosh, 1992). The problem with oppression is
not the oppressed, it is the oppressor. Once the social construction of the
oppressor status is made invisible, the oppressor can no longer draw privilege at
the expense of others based on their loyalty or the perception of their loyalty to
the oppressive system. In this way the system of oppression is abolished. In a
related work, a book entitled, *How the Irish Became White* (Ignatiev, 1996), the
author asked Whites, in particular the Irish, to consider why they stopped being
ethnic and became "White." The author challenges the notion of "White" as a
social membership group by deconstructing it, by asking what White and
whiteness really are. He added to this challenge by calling into question the
etiology and purpose of the concept of whiteness and by asking what the
political, economic, social incentives and costs to those who were ethnic, who
were Irish, Italian, French, German, and so forth were, in "becoming White," and
in largely ceasing to be ethnic. Although the *Race Traitor* philosophy, like all
philosophies, is not a perfect one, it has opened up the dialogue on race as a

social construction exponentially and it is provoking thought and action toward the deconstruction and eventual eradication of race to move in new and different directions.

In the seminars that Arboleda conducts following what is in essence a dramatic and comedic performance of his autobiography (see the blurb in the inside front cover of the text), he makes his own such contribution to radically opening up the dialogue on race as a social construction. He leads his audience in socially reconstructing the identities of many famous people assumed to be monoracial, despite even their own proclamation otherwise, as multicultural. For example, golfer Tiger Woods, who despite repeatedly stating that he is of Asian, Black, Native American or American Indian, and European ancestry, and culturally more Asian than anything else, is referred to in the media as only Black; actress Halle Berry, who acknowledges her biracial ancestry (Black father and White mother) but identifies Black, and who credits her White mother with helping her to develop a sense of herself as culturally Black, is also referred to as only Black; and football player Brett Favre, who although he looks most like his Irish mother is, he states, more culturally akin to his Native American father, is referred to as only White (McCormick & Begley, 1996). In taking his audience on this journey to deconstruct the monolithic nature of the notion of racial identity, Arboleda encourages them to rethink their identities, the assumptions they make about themselves and others based on appearance, socially constructed family histories, terroristically ravaged family ancestries, privileges and entitlements that are taken for granted, are denied, or that at some future point could be stripped or afforded (Takaki, 1993). Arboleda begs the question: What if tomorrow someone thinks that you are not what you are (Straight if you are Gay) or that you are what your are not (Latina if you are a White woman) and as a result your access to participation in democracy changes for the better, you are welcomed where never before, or for the worse, you are barred from participating in what you had previously been welcomed to participate; what will you do? Does it have to affect us personally before we are compelled to take a stand?

RACIAL IDENTITY DEVELOPMENT THEORY

Racial Identity Development Theory emerged in the 1950s and continues to evolve today (Clark & O'Donnell, 1999a). Models of Black and then White racial identity development emerged first. Although there are slight variations in the conceptualizations of both the Black and White models, the following review of them is more or less representative of a composite model for each racial identity. Both Black Identity Development (Cross, 1973, 1978; Jackson, 1976a, 1976b; Jackson & Hardiman, 1988) and White Identity Development (Bollin & Finkel, 1995; Bonnett, 1996; Bowser & Hunt, 1981; Dennis, 1981; Feagin & Vera, 1995; Fishkin, 1995; Frankenberg, 1993a, 1993b; Goldberg, 1990, 1993a, 1993b; Grundmann; 1994; Hardiman, 1979, 1982; Hardiman & Jackson, 1992; Helms, 1984, 1990a, 1990b, 1995; Kantrowitz, 1996; Katz, 1978; Karp, 1981; Keating, 1995; Stowe, 1996; Terry, 1981; Wellman, 1993, 1996) models suggest that there are four major stages in the racial identity development of Black and White Americans, respectively.

Black Identity Development

For Black Americans these four stages are as follows: Stage One: Acceptance of Racism, Stage Two: Resistance to Racism, Stage Three: Redirection, and Stage Four: Internalization (Cross, 1973, 1978; Jackson, 1976a, 1976b; Jackson & Hardiman, 1988).

The model argues that all Black Americans, by virtue of their socialization in the institutionally racist United States, come to some degree very early on in life even infancy perhaps, to accept racism. The politics of skin color in the Black American community, as articulated in, *The Sweeter the Juice* (Haizlip, 1994), is an excellent example of this acceptance. The authors describe how the racist norms of beauty, desirability, intelligence, and access that White American society constructs around concrete, visual whiteness are acculturated to by Black Americans and recreated within Black social order: "high yellow," "light eyes," "good hair," "house Negro," and so forth. According to the model, one is born into this stage and may function within it for one's whole life.

Movement into subsequent stages is developmental and may occur in one of two ways; either via informal experiences, circumstantial usually traumatic, highly emotionally charged events that have consciousness shattering impact, or, via formal experiences, deliberate interaction designed to influence attitudes and/or behavior. Informal experiences are more likely the catalysts in engendering movement from stage one to stage two, whereas formal experiences are more likely the catalysts in producing movement beyond stage two (Cross, 1973, 1978; Jackson, 1976a, 1976b; Jackson & Hardiman, 1988).

For example, a Black man in accepting racism may imagine that he can avoid the evils of racism by "acting White," becoming well-educated, a Harvard lawyer, using or learning only narrowly defined White or so-called standard English, and adopting so-called White upper-class, (a) employment values (becoming a prosecutor on a crusade to put *Black* criminals in jail), (b) behavioral norms (promoting country line dancing while attacking rap music), and, (c) recreational toys (attaining membership in a formerly all-White country club); doing "the Clarence Thomas," so to speak. Then one day, driving home from work, this man is stopped in his own neighborhood by a police officer, questioned as to what he is doing in "this" neighborhood, and then beaten severely for "obviously lying" about living there; given the proverbial "Negro wake-up call," no matter how well you play the game, eventually you will be reminded that you are not a full participant in it (Cross, 1973, 1978; Jackson, 1976a, 1976b; Jackson & Hardiman, 1988).

This circumstantial, traumatic event causes this man, almost overnight, to rethink his whole existence. He sees how naive he has been and becomes vehemently incensed, mad at his own short-sightedness. In short, he moves into resisting racism, perhaps he joins the Nation of Islam. Here the man shifts from identifying himself congruently with White society to identifying himself in opposition to it. Although acceptance and resistance seem like diametrically opposed stages, there is one significant common element to both stages, an individual in either stage still defines her or himself in relationship to the dominant group, either congruent with or incongruent with White society's order (Cross, 1973, 1978; Jackson, 1976a, 1976b; Jackson & Hardiman, 1988).

Once some of the anger subsides, if it does, this man may begin to seek out ways to redirect his energies in defining himself, for the first time, as separate and distinct from Whiteness; not to please White society nor to show indignance toward it, but rather, attempting to allow it to have no impact, positive or negative, at all. This man is no longer at the mercy of chance to influence his stage movement here, rather he seeks out opportunities that may have the effect of assisting him in moving. Perhaps this man attends the Million Man March, is inspired to get involved in his community at home afterward, and joins a group like *100 Black Men of America, Inc.* (see Part III) to work to help young Black men to achieve, not with blind deference to sociopolitical realities nor with debilitating animosity toward them, but with healthy critical consciousness and reliance on community. The ideal here is Black for Black (Cross, 1973, 1978; Jackson, 1976a, 1976b; Jackson & Hardiman, 1988).

As a consequence of working on this endeavor, this individual finds it necessary to accept an appointment to a Board of Directors of a predominantly White organization whose political support he is working to secure for *100 Black Men of America, Inc.* He has to work with many non-Blacks, mostly Whites, as a result of this choice. Consequently, he sets out to facilitate the movement of the whole board through the model in an effort to impact at least this one group's entrenched racism. In so engaging himself, the man has now moved into internalization. He works with all the individuals on the board, the few Blacks and the many Whites, all presumably at different levels within the Black Identity Development model and similar White Identity Development model, toward the end of eventually aiding their entry into internalization as well. As a consequence of work in this context, this individual comes to integrate his racial identity with all of his other identities vis-à-vis socioeconomic class background, gender, sexual preference or orientation, and so forth. He comes to connect with the multicultural paradigm, with no longer necessarily prioritizing one aspect of his identity or his social justice work over any others, but rather fighting for social justice on all discriminatory fronts in a holistic fashion (Cross, 1973, 1978; Jackson, 1976a, 1976b; Jackson & Hardiman, 1988).

White Identity Development

For White Americans, the four stages are as follows; Stage One: Acceptance of Racism (where acceptance may be active, initiating a racist act, or passive, going along with a racist act), Stage Two: Resistance to Racism (where resistance may be passive, avoiding a racist act, or active, confronting a racist act), Stage Three: Redefinition, and Stage Four: Internalization (Hardiman, 1979, 1982; Hardiman & Jackson, 1988; Helms, 1984, 1990a, 1990b, 1995). Because the Black and

White models are similar, the following is a slightly more abbreviated explanation of the White model than was offered previously of the Black one. In particular, what is articulated about the White model are the subtle but important ways in which it differs from the Black one.

The White model argues that all White Americans, by virtue of their socialization in the institutionally racist United States, come to some degree very early on in life even infancy perhaps, to actively and passively accept racism (telling [active] or just listening to [passive] a racist joke; burning a cross on the front yard of a Black person [active] or simply not doing anything to stop someone from doing this [passive]—although clearly there exists a continuum between active and passive, it is important to remember that one person's active is another person's passive; the degree of activeness or passiveness perceived by an individual is a function of the degree of their consciousness of racism). According to the model, one is born into this stage and may function within it for one's whole life (Hardiman, 1979, 1982; Hardiman & Jackson, 1988; Helms, 1984, 1990a, 1990b, 1995).

Movement into subsequent stages here is the same as in the Black model. It is developmental and may occur in one of two ways; either via informal experiences (circumstantial, usually traumatic, highly emotionally charged events that have consciousness-shattering impact), or, via formal experiences (deliberate interaction designed to influence attitudes and/or behavior). Informal experiences are more likely the catalysts in engendering movement from stage one to stage two (someone in the acceptance of racism stage does not generally enroll in a racism awareness seminar unless they are mandated to do so), whereas formal experiences are more likely the catalysts in producing movement beyond stage two (Hardiman, 1979, 1982; Hardiman & Jackson,1988; Helms, 1984, 1990a, 1990b, 1995).

A circumstantial, traumatic event causes an individual, almost overnight, to rethink her whole existence. She sees how naive she has been and becomes incensed, angry at her own short-sightedness. In short, she moves into resisting racism; first passively and then later, if the rethinking and associated anger persist, perhaps more actively (Hardiman, 1979, 1982; Hardiman & Jackson, 1988; Helms, 1984, 1990a, 1990b, 1995).

Once some of the anger subsides, *if* it does, the individual may begin to seek out ways to redefine her racial identity not as only good (a characteristic of a person in the acceptance stage—as better than others, consciously or subconsciously) or as only bad (a characteristic of a person at the resistance stage—as worse than others though often still, at least subconsciously, acting as though one is better than others) but an integration of both good and bad in such a way that one finally owns the privilege one enjoys whether or not one wants it at the same time that one works with the deepest commitment toward the eradication of that privilege (Hardiman, 1979, 1982; Hardiman & Jackson, 1988; Helms, 1984, 1990a, 199b, 1995).

Movement into *internalization* occurs when the individual is able to integrate her racial identity with all of her other identities vis-à-vis socioeconomic class background, gender, sexual preference or orientation, and so forth. At this stage, the individual is committed to facilitating other people's movement through the model (Hardiman, 1979, 1982; Hardiman & Jackson, 1988; Helms, 1984, 1990a, 1990b, 1995).

Critique and Expansion of the Black and White Identity Development Models

The major critique of the models is that they are linear, modernistic, and positivistic (Kinchloe, Pinar, & Slattery, 1994; Hidalgo, Chávez Chávez, & Ramage, 1996). But, however limiting they may be in this regard they are also liberating. In particular, they give students a conceptual framework for understanding race and racial identity; something to point to and say, "See, this is what I mean" (Clark, 1999, p. 103). They also help students to think about their own consciousness vis-à-vis race in very specific ways. For example, once students understand the basic concepts of the models they are able to manipulate them in ways that at least challenge their linear and developmental orientation, if not eradicate it. In so doing, one can look at the models and ask whether or not an individual's consciousness can be at more than one stage simultaneously (can Nation of Islam membership occur at stage two and/or stage three depending on how this membership is viewed by the individual member?), or whether or not two people exhibiting similar behavior can be analyzed in terms of their consciousness in engaging in that behavior as at different stages (is interracial dating *always* "jungle fever" or can it be done with dignity?), and so forth (Clark, 1999).

More recently, other models have been developed in an attempt to describe patterns of racial identity development among Latinas and Latinos, Puerto Ricans in particular (Banks, 1992; Flores, 1993; Gay, 1985), Native Americans or American Indians, Navajos in particular (Banks, 1992; Gay, 1985; Márquez, 1996), and Asians, Chinese and Southeast Asians in particular (Ang, 1995; Banks, 1992; Bhachu, 1996; Gay, 1985; Said, 1985). Although these models are more similar to the Black Identity Development model than the White one, they are also different from it; describing, in varied measure, both experiences shared by all People of Color in the United States as well as experiences unique to each group. Most notably, these latter models deal with second language issues not addressed by the by the Black one.[4] The Navajo model, the most divergent, challenges the notion that identity is linear, arguing instead that it is circular, and adds a spiritual component to it.[5]

In the mid 1980s, Omi and Winant (1994), developed a more integrated perspective of what they called "racial formation" in the United States. In developing their perspective they offer a description of the concept of race that embodies the complexity Arboleda's experiences require:

> There is a continuous temptation to think of race as an *essence*, as something fixed, concrete, and objective. And there is also an opposite temptation: to imagine race as a mere *illusion*, a purely ideological construct which some ideal non-racist social order would eliminate. It is necessary to challenge both these positions, to disrupt and reframe the rigid and bipolar manner in which they are

posed and debated, and to transcend the presumably irreconcilable relationship between them.

The effort must be made to understand race as an unstable and "decentered" complex of social meanings constantly being transformed by political struggle. With this in mind, let us propose a definition: *race is a concept which signifies and symbolizes social conflicts and interests by referring to different types of human bodies.* (Omi & Winant, 1994, pp. 54–55)

With this conceptualization of race in mind, Omi and Winant go on to describe how they believe racial identity is thus formed:

We define *racial formation* as the sociohistorical process by which racial categories are created, inhabited, transformed, and destroyed. . . . racial formation is a process of historically situated *projects* in which human bodies and social structures are represented and organized. . . . we link racial formation to the evolution of hegemony, the way in which society is organized and ruled. . . . From a racial formation perspective, race is a matter of both social structure and cultural representation. Too often, the attempt is made to understand race simply or primarily in terms of only one of these two analytical dimensions.

. . . Conversely, many examinations of racial difference—understood as a matter of cultural attributes *a la* ethnicity theory, or as a society-wide signification system, *a la* some poststructuralist accounts—cannot comprehend such structural phenomena as racial stratification in the labor market or patterns of residential segregation.

An alternative approach is to think of racial formation processes as occurring through a linkage between structure and representation. Racial *projects* do the ideological "work" of making these links. *A racial project is simultaneously an interpretation, representation, or explanation of racial dynamics, and an effort to reorganize and redistribute resources along particular racial lines.* Racial projects connect what race *means* in a particular discursive practice and the ways in which both social structures and everyday experiences are racially *organized*, based on that meaning. (Omi & Winant, 1994, pp. 55–56)

It is important to point out that although the vast majority of racial identity development theory is based in U.S. sociopolitics, most of Arboleda's identity was developed in relationship to sociopolitics operating outside the United States (although still clearly heavily influenced by those endemic to the United States). This is a clear shortcoming of racial identity development theory and the ability it has to facilitate our understanding of Arboleda's experiences.[6] At the same time, because Arboleda's struggle is, at least at the current historical moment, to make a place for himself vis-à-vis his "multiethnic, multicultural, 'multiracial'" identity inside the United States, racial identity development theory can offer us some insight into Arboleda's complex sociocultural, sociopolitical, and psychosocial endeavor to have his voice heard in the current domestic debate of race politics.

And, Arboleda is not alone in having to either force-fit or pick-and-choose elements of the various models of racial identity development to try and describe his experiences. People of mixed backgrounds generally find that they have more in common with the Of Color models than the White ones, namely because they, like People of Color, must deal with the reality that their reality is not *the* reality acknowledged in the mainstream, the floor tile is green not blue (Ang, 1995; Banks, 1992; Bhachu, 1996; Bollin & Finkel, 1995; Bonnett, 1996; Bowser & Hunt, 1981; Cross, 1973, 1978; Dennis, 1981; Feagin & Vera, 1995; Fishkin, 1995; Flores, 1993; Frankenberg, 1993a, 1993b; Gay, 1985; Goldberg, 1990, 1993a, 1993b; Grundmann; 1994; Hardiman, 1979, 1982; Hardiman & Jackson, 1992; Helms, 1984, 1990a, 1990b, 1995; Jackson, 1976a, 1976b; Jackson & Hardiman, 1988; Kantrowitz, 1996; Katz, 1978; Karp, 1981; Keating, 1995; Macedo & Bartolomé, in press; Márquez, 1996; Mura, 1991; Said, 1985; Stowe, 1996; Terry, 1981; Wellman, 1993, 1996). Despite this, the identity development experiences of mixed race peoples in the United States are perhaps even more complex than those of People of Color with only one racial group membership (Haizlip, 1994). This is because mixed race people are often put in a position to have to choose one aspect of their identity in order to "fit" into either the "White" mainstream (pass), or to "fit" into the Native America or American Indian, Black, Latina and Latino, or Asian mainstream (Haney López, 1996; Omi & Winant, 1994). They are rarely permitted to maintain dual or multiple identities in either White or Of Color communities. At the same time, when they do make a choice they are criticized for whichever choice they make (Haizlip, 1994; Omi & Winant, 1994). There are, however, some significant differences in the dynamics of power based on which choice is, in fact, made. Either choice reinforces racial reification, but the choice to pass for "White" is an act of "border terrorism" (a concept that will be discussed in greater detail in an ensuing section of this chapter under the heading "Racial Borderlands" (Clark, 1997), whereas the choice to claim a single Of Color identity is an act of resistance to assimilation, however limiting (Clark, 1997; McLaren, 1995). If one is not claiming all of whom one is, then one is still allowing those in power (who insist first, on racial categorization and second, on single category racial categorization) to force one into making a choice (not only checking a box, but checking only one box), compartmentalizing one's identity (Haney López, 1996). This is another example of the persistent negative influence of modernism on racial identity, *either* you are this *or* you are that (Dussell, 1993; McGowan, 1991; Rattansi, 1994; Rosaldo, 1993; Smart, 1992; Young, 1990). The postmodern response might be, you can be both, many, neither, none; it is all in how one chooses to identify. But, as Omi and Winant (1994) point out, the notion of freedom of choice, even with respect to something as personal as individual identity, is limited by the complex sociopolitical context in which that choice is being made.

As alluded to previously, People of Color buy into the modernistic construct of either/or as much as White people do when they limit how people in their own communities may define themselves in order to secure community acceptance (Fordham, 1988; Ogbu, 1986). This is done when the range of choices from which individuals may choose in attempting to define their identities are constructed as *either* culturally normative and acceptable, that is "Native American or American Indian," "Black," "Latina and Latino," and "Asian," *or* as culturally nonnormative and not acceptable, ultimately culturally traitorous even when such does not involve "border terrorism," but rather embodies the "border crossing as liberation" spirit (another concept that will be discussed in greater detail in an ensuing section of this chapter under the heading "Racial Borderlands; Clark, 1997; Fordham, 1988; Ogbu, 1986).

Conversely, White people do not limit other White people in defining their self-concept[7] as much as they limit how and to what degree People of Color who choose to "pass" may define themselves and, based on their definition, how much compartmentalized access to participation in democracy they will be afforded as previously discussed. To a large extent, the choice and ability to "pass" are highly correlated with the politics of skin color (Haizlip, 1994). And this has been the case for longer than the United States has existed (Takaki, 1993). Since its inception, under the auspices of slavery, light skinned enslaved Africans were given incremental "privilege" that dark skinned enslaved Africans were not, hence the emergence of the terms and corresponding concepts, "house Negroes" and "field Negroes" (Haizlip, 1994). This was followed by the paper bag, the door, and the blue vein tests (Haizlip, 1994). These tests set the standard for "passing." If one was as light as or lighter than a paper bag on hand at an establishment or the color of the wood of the door of an establishment one was permitted entrée. The blue vein test required that the blue color of the veins in the underside of one's wrist be discernible to be afforded access.

The terrible current day impact of past racist practices *within* Of Color communities is profound. The influence of whiteness as "bad" is manifest as jealousy and/or hatred within Of Color communities, where lighter skinned members are often seen as not dark enough because they are sometimes able to access benefits darker skinned members cannot, and/or they are seen as constant reminders of the brutal history of enslavement, colonization, internment, and so forth; the rape of the enslaved, colonized, interned woman by the White slave owner, colonizer, interner, the guarantors of White supremacy (Brown, 1971; Douglas, 1972; Franklin, 1966; Haizlip, 1994; Takaki, 1993). But, perhaps ironically, the influence of whiteness as "good" can also be seen within Of Color communities manifest as internalized self-hatred, where particularly dark skinned members are often characterized as *too* dark, meaning not attractive (Haizlip, 1994).

Perhaps most destructively, People of Color, in socially constructing parameters that limit the range of culturally acceptable expressions of identity within their communities have led many young people in these communities to believe that getting an education is "acting White," so in order to "be" Native American or American Indian, Black, Latina and Latino, or Asian, one must eschew even a comprehensive multiculturally conceptualized education, one of the most reliable and viable means of increasing one's access to participation in democracy (Fordham, 1988; Macedo & Bartolomé, in press; Ogbu, 1986). This not only debilitates People of Color by reinforcing their marginalization, reinforcing the limiting nature of racism, it also facilitates Whites in maintaining their status quo (Morrison, 1992; Nakayama & Krizek, 1995;

Novick, 1995; Powell, 1996; Roediger, 1991, 1994; Stowe, 1996; Terry, 1981; Young, 1990; Zinn, 1970). The delimiting counteraction, the antiracist response, is for both Of Color and White communities to embrace mixed raced people in their multidimensional histories and further, for mixed raced people to likewise embrace themselves, their whole selves (Haney López, 1996; McIntosh, 1989, 1992; Omi & Winant, 1994; Thompson, 1996).

The most recent U.S. Census report indicates that 20,000 people identified as People of Color in their birth records disappear from the population annually. That is, they do not die nor immigrate. Rather, it is suspected that they have had their birth and other vital records changed to reflect a White identity (Haney López, 1996). And although part of this phenomenon may be attributable to internalized self-hatred, certainly the very real differences in access to participation in democracy afforded Whites, or people perceived to be White is also at issue here (Delgado, 1995; McIntosh, 1989, 1992). What a masterful job (no pun intended) the ideology of White supremacy has done on both People of Color and Whites, when People of Color self-police, in the absence of White policing, to limit their own choices in identity development and the thoughts and actions that derive from it (Fordham, 1998; Macedo & Bartolomé, in press; Morrison, 1992; Ogbu, 1986).

But, what about mixed people who do not fit visually anywhere; people like Arboleda who cannot or who would at best have an awkward time trying to pass for White or any single Of Color group; people whom, like Arboleda, may resent other mixed people who can and sometimes also choose to try and fit into a single racial identity group? It is this group of people who perhaps reject the construct of race the most (Omi & Winant, 1994). Compare the experiences of Arboleda and his brother. Because Arboleda's brother is darker than Arboleda, he cannot even try to pass for White (conversely Arboleda tries to pass for Italian, chap. 19), therefore he has fewer choices about how to identify then Arboleda, and he also confronts fewer contradictions in his racial identity development. As a young child, Arboleda comes home from school wanting to be White, but his brother never does (chap. 7). These are but a few examples of the added complexities of not only being mixed but "looking" mixed. Depending on the degree of sun-tanning such a person has done, they could be "anything," at the same time feeling as though they are at once everything and nothing (Anzaldua, 1987; Fanon, 1967; Fishkin, 1995; Hall 1991a).

These contradictions and the emotional anguish they cause mixed people lead to the negative characterization of mixed marriages or committed relationships as doomed to "failure" because of race, and mixed children as mixed up because they have no race (Haizlip, 1994). It is not the issue of race viewed either as a reification or a construct that makes marriages or committed relationships "fail,"[8] or that makes mixed children struggle with issues of racial identity development. Rather, it is how the issue of race is wielded in society (Omi & Winant, 1994). In Arboleda's experience, society has wielded race in very negative ways. According to Arboleda, his paternal grandmother, in internalizing Black self-hatred, in becoming fugitive (Giroux, 1996) of her blackness by buying into the reification of inferiority and superiority based on racial group membership, comes to believe that by marrying a Filipino/Chinese she is marrying "up" (chapter 2). The same argument might also apply to Arboleda's father and Arboleda himself.

Conversely, Arboleda's mother's decision to marry "down" can also be seen as a function of the negative wielding of race in society (and the society she grew up in was Hitler's Germany), as the social construction of the "Other" and darkness as "exotic," "sexual," and so forth (Omi & Winant, 1994). Arboleda's mother may superficially suggest that her own lightness is not as attractive as Arboleda's father's darkness, she may superficially engage in pseudo White Shamanism (Johnson, 1995; Rose, 1992), professing the desire to be an "Other" under the auspices of it being more aesthetically pleasing (chaps. 4, 5, & 7). Ultimately however, she leaves the marriage when her comfort zone as an "Other" goes beyond the aesthetic, when she is faced with the persistent and pervasive alienating nature of the sociopolitical reality of being "Other."

The wisdom in Arboleda's experience is not derived from his consciously articulated plea to do away with race whether as a reification or a construct. Rather, it is derived from his implicitly expressed plea, echoing the words of Omi and Winant (1994), that the complex sociopolitical dynamics negatively impacting people because of race or the perception of race be interrogated, challenged, and ultimately eradicated so that all of who each individual is can be claimed in a liberatory fashion.

RACIAL POWER DYNAMICS

Underlying all of the discussion in this guide is the assertion that certain people, based on social group memberships or the presumption of social group memberships (e.g., the ability to "pass") have greater access to participation in democracy. This assertion comes from the power + prejudice = "ism" equation (Jackson, 1976b). This equation argues that although all people have prejudice, in the case most relevant to Arboleda's story, race prejudice, not all people have access to power at the institutional level in society to enforce these prejudices; those who do create "isms," in this case racism. Racial prejudice and racism are distinguished from each other by the institutional power associated with the latter but not with the former (Laing & Cooper, 1971; Loewen, 1995; Novick, 1995; Oakes, 1985; Powell, 1996; Seldon, 1992; Spring, 1997; Takaki, 1993; Zinn, 1970, 1980). By virtue of being White and by virtue of the fact that Whites have and historically have had disproportionate access to institutional power in the United States, the racial prejudice toward People of Color that all Whites are socialized, consciously and unconsciously, to essentially embrace is necessarily entrenched in and enforced as racism via our political, economic, and social structures (Laing & Cooper, 1971; Loewen, 1995; Novick, 1995; Oakes, 1985; Powell, 1996; Seldon, 1992; Spring, 1997; Takaki, 1993; Zinn, 1970, 1980). According to this equation, seemingly parallel actions on the part of a White person and a Person of Color have different impact because of the power issue. For example, for a White person to be called a "honky" by a Person of Color is simply not the same thing as that White person calling a Person of Color a "nigger" or a "spic." The White person's actions are reinforced exponentially by the racism of the superstructure while those of a Person of Color toward that White person are not; hence the latter carries less weight, less impact (Laing & Cooper, 1971; Loewen, 1995; Novick, 1995; Oakes, 1985; Powell, 1996; Seldon, 1992; Spring, 1997; Takaki, 1993; Zinn, 1970, 1980). Consequently, People of Color are denied or afforded less access to participation in democracy, whereas Whites are granted or afforded greater access (Laing & Cooper, 1971; Loewen, 1995; Novick, 1995; Oakes, 1985; Powell, 1996; Seldon, 1992; Spring, 1997; Takaki, 1993; Zinn, 1970, 1980). And it is important to note that this is the case whether or not one wants it be so. By simply willing oneself to try and gain greater access or by attempting to give up the disproportionately greater access one enjoys, one is not necessarily successful in the endeavor, not individually or, more importantly, institutionally—nor in fundamentally changing the way institutionalized opportunity structures are configured to reproduce differential access (Laing & Cooper, 1971; Loewen, 1995; Novick, 1995; Oakes, 1985; Powell, 1996; Seldon, 1992; Spring, 1997; Takaki, 1993; Zinn, 1970, 1980).

Unfortunately, this equation can lead, in particular, well-intentioned Whites to over-identify People of Color as victims in such a way that it takes their agency away. The equation argues that because both Whites and People of Color so resist seeing the persistent, pervasive, and perilous *institutional* nature of racism (and other forms of discrimination), it is necessary to make such audaciously clear to them by creating what is perhaps an all too perfect dichotomy between the haves and have-nots so to speak, in an effort to get them to see and ultimately own the reality of inequity. bell hooks sums up the cost of such oversimplifying practice in *Killing Rage: Ending Racism* (1995):

> . . . those black folks who embrace victim identity do so because they find it mediates relations with whites, that it is easier to make appeals that call for sympathy rather than redress and reparations. As long as white Americans are more willing to extend concern and care to black folks who have a "victim-focused black identity," a shift in paradigms will not take place. (p. 58)

In considering the social reality of victim identification, it is important to recognize that, in actuality, Whites are far better at claiming victim status than are People of Color (one could make the parallel argument for all members of overrepresented social membership groups, for example, native speakers of English, the upper middle- and upper-class, men, and so forth; Clark, 1999; Welsing, 1970). An excellent example of this can be found in the observation made by a man who was a student in a class taught in a prison in Massachusetts. In the discussion of some aspect of women's oppression, he asked the rhetorical question, "How come when something bad happens to a White woman she is shown crying about it all over the news, but when the same thing or even something worse happens to a Woman of Color we do not hear about it or if we do, we almost never see *her* cry?" This observation should now lead us to ask ourselves, "*Who* is playing the victim?" (Clark, 1999; Welsing, 1970).

It is also important to address the way in which the racial power dynamics between Whites and People of Color infect relationships within and between Groups of Color (Allen, 1994; Bowles & Gintis, 1977; Chasnoff & Cohen, 1996; Goldberg, 1993a, 1993b; Lipsitz, 1995; Macedo & Bartolomé, in press; Saxton, 1991). To do this we have to take a step back and consider the larger sociopolitical etiology in which all of these dynamics have emerged. Racial power dynamics are but one kind of power dynamics operating to preserve the status quo. There are also power dynamics based on socioeconomic class, gender, and so forth (Allen, 1994; Bowles & Gintis, 1977; Chasnoff & Cohen, 1996; Goldberg, 1993a, 1993b; Lipsitz, 1995; Macedo & Bartolomé, in press; Saxton, 1991; Warner 1993). Taken in their entirety, these dynamics represent the way in which a population is divided, conquered, colonized and then managed toward the ends of those in power (Allen, 1994; Bowles & Gintis, 1977; Chasnoff & Cohen, 1996; Goldberg, 1993a, 1993b; Lipsitz, 1995; Macedo & Bartolomé, in press; Saxton, 1991). If the oppressed can be encouraged to fight amongst themselves for what amounts to crumbs, they will never notice the five-course meal on the table of the oppressor (Allen, 1994; Bowles & Gintis, 1977; Chasnoff & Cohen, 1996; Goldberg, 1993a, 1993b; Lipsitz, 1995; Macedo & Bartolomé, in press; Saxton, 1991). Clearly then, the impact of the manipulation of these dynamics is violent (Bourdieu, Passeron, DeSaint Martin, & Teese, 1996). But where does this violence begin? (Spring, 1997).

When we speak of this violence, we must be clear about whether we are, in fact, speaking about violence—that initiated by the oppressor, or whether we are speaking about the reactive violence of the oppressed (Freire, 1970). We must also be clear about of what form of violence or reactive violence we speak: the physical, the economic, the political, or the psychological. Violence can take all of these forms. For example, there is institutionalized militarism, like the Rodney King beating (the physical); institutionalized classism, like that which would have denied Rodney King access to equal representation under the law because of an inability to pay had his beating not been videotaped and viewed nationally (the economic); institutionalized racism, like the jury verdict on the cops who beat Rodney King (the political); and an institutionalized standard of what constitutes "normal" behavior that leads to the pathologicalization of the oppressed, like the notion that a stumbling drunk Rodney King, in his bigness, Blackness, and maleness, somehow posed a threat to several not so small, White, male cops armed with billy clubs and guns, hence leading an almost all White jury to rationalize their actions (the psychological; Clark, 1993a; Delgado, 1995; Gooding-Williams, 1993). Reactive violence can only take the form of the physical and, of course, only in a noninstitutionalized fashion because, as suggested previously, the oppressed, by definition, lack access to the structural means, the power, to institutionalize their prejudices into a legislative, executive, and judicial system of government or, in this and many past historical moments, of control (Clark, 1993a; Delgado, 1995; Gooding-Williams, 1993).

When the oppressor initiates nonphysical violence (economic, political, and/or psychological) toward the oppressed it is constructed as "symbolic" violence. Eurocentric education is a good example of this so-called "symbolic" violence (Bourdieu, Passeron, DeSaint Martin, & Teese, 1996), only there is nothing "symbolic" about it, not in its initiation or impact. On the contrary, real, live, thinking, feeling, and acting human beings who existed, exist, and will continue to exist, do so not merely as objects in relationship to unowned events that have mysteriously affected them, but as subjects, authors of and affecting their own events, while simultaneously engaging in a cold war about representation, access to participation, in democracy, being waged at a very violent level of physiological, economic, psychological, and spiritual survival (Clark, 1993a; Delgado, 1995; Gooding-Williams, 1993).

So, the oppressors initiate violence and the oppressed respond with violence. The oppressors then initiate more violence and the vicious cycle is begun. But, there is another dimension to flesh out here, perhaps what can be called a "sub-cycle." As postulated earlier, when the oppressed prey on each other with violence, is that initiating or responding with violence? It is a response to the violence initiated by the oppressors but it is a displaced response. "Submerged in reality, the oppressed cannot perceive clearly the 'order' which serves the interest of the oppressors . . . Chafing under the restrictions of this order, they often manifest a type of horizontal violence . . ." (Freire, 1970, p. 48). The media represents this kind of violence as "racial" because occasionally it occurs between different racial and ethnic groups. But the majority of the time, this violence occurs within a racial or ethnic group (Giroux, 1996). This then would not be "racial" violence, unless perhaps the conflict arose around color gradations within a group as discussed in reference to Haizlip (1994), previously, yet it is represented as such because the predominantly White media, while it does not see itself as racial or ethnic, sees all People of Color this way. Hence, violence between Whites is just violence, but violence between Blacks or Latinas and Latinos or Asians or Native Peoples is constructed as "racial violence" (Clark, Jenkins, & Stowers, in press).

Recently, all of these arguments about institutional racism (including the power plus prejudice equation), agency, victimization (as just discussed), and the decentering of whiteness (as discussed in the previous section of this chapter) have been radically challenged (Clark, 1999; hooks, 1993). The challenge is directed at the power-plus-prejudice equation and the way this equation references institutional racism. Although inherent in the challenge is a clear understanding the power relations these concepts are employed to describe, the challenge suggests that focusing the description of power relations around these concepts can, at least inadvertently, create the perception that when say, for example, young Latino and Black males kill each other, it is somehow less important than when Whites kill People of Color, or when agents of the state (cops) kill People of Color (Clark, 1999; Bourdieu, Passeron, DeSaint Martin, & Teese, 1996; Hutchinson, 1994; Kunjufu, 1995; Laing & Cooper, 1971). Certainly, the political right has made it clear that nothing is an epidemic until it negatively impacts the White middle-class (Jenkins, 1994). But the challenge does not focus critique on the right, rather the left. In essence, it argues that when the left, especially the White left, employ these concepts in an attempt to advocate on behalf of People of Color, they actually encourage the diminution of the source of greatest immediate destruction in Of Color communities, young Men of Color allied against each other in gangs (Jenkins, 1994). Clearly, as alluded to previously, in working with Whites one should be concerned about how easy it is for Whites to view the problems in Of Color communities as the fault of those who reside in these communities and disavow themselves of any responsibility (Hardiman, 1979, 1982; Helms, 1990a, 1990b, 1995). Refocusing Whites on the root of the problem as institutional racism is an important part of getting them to invest themselves in the change process (Hardiman, 1979, 1982; Helms, 1990a, 1990b, 1995). Typically, this process has focused on eroding the opportunity structures that prevent People of Color from accessing positions of power; positions where the decisions about the prioritization and allocation of resources for education, housing, health care, and employment to Of Color communities are made (Loewen, 1995; Novick, 1995; Powell, 1996). Again, inherent in the challenge is a clear understanding of all of these dynamics as well, yet, the sense of it is that to focus efforts on addressing change at this level once again diverts attention away from the immediacy of the need for change at the grassroots level in Of Color communities (Clark, 1999). The challenge goes on to articulate the sense that the White left's focus on institutional instead of individual racism, and especially, intragroup racial prejudice manifest as life-threatening hostility at the community level, is but another way to recenter discussion around Whiteness (Clark, 1999). And in a deeply provocative way this is right. It puts Whites at the center again, not as the good guys but as the bad guys which may be how the White left manifests its racist pathology to be at the center (Clark, 1999).

It is hard to come to any comfortable resolution regarding racial power dynamics and how to understand them. Perhaps most important in the effort to effect real change in them is in remaining uncomfortable and unresolved about them. Within this nagging unfinishedness may emerge the lived everyday commitment to work to create change (Omi & Winant, 1994).

RACIAL BORDERLANDS

Most people may have never thought about borders in any sense other than the physical, like a fence or property demarcation, a football gridiron, a state line, or international boundary. But borders may also be conceptualized in the psychological, emotional, social, political, and cultural sense among others (Giroux, 1992a). Expanding thought regarding borders in these ways, we can imagine a person like Arboleda.

In the context of emergent academic discourse regarding this reconceptualization of borders, what is called border pedagogy, Arboleda's life experiences, as a person who does not "fit" into the so-called mainstream or "center," (the, simplistically, White, Anglo Saxon, Protestant male middle around which everyone else is forced, to varying degrees and in various ways, to conform) become an obvious example of an "Other," living in the margin(s), on the border(s) (Angus, 1990; Anzaldua, 1987; Clark, 1997; Clark & O'Donnell, 1999b; Connolly & Noumair, 1997; Giroux, 1992a; hooks, 1993; Thompson, 1996; Wellman, 1996). And Arboleda, perhaps even more so than many "Others" from traditionally underrepresented social membership groups (especially racial and ethnic ones), because he is not only not able to "pass" as a member of the dominant group but because he is also not easily able to pass as a member of any *single* traditionally underrepresented group. As a result, he is, perhaps, more marginalized, confronts more borders than even most "Others" do on a daily basis.

As a speaker of English with native fluency he can find part of himself in the center, as a person with economic means he can find part of himself in the center, as a man he can find part of himself in the center, as a heterosexual he can find part of himself in the center, and as an able-bodied person he can find part of himself in the center. But, in finding parts of himself in the center, he also finds other parts of himself, his mixed race, his mixed ethnicity, his mixed marriage, his commitment to interrupting and challenging racism, and so forth, marginalized, decentered, relegated to the borderlands (Angus, 1990; Anzaldua, 1987; Clark, 1997; Clark & O'Donnell, 1999b; Connolly & Noumair, 1997; Giroux, 1992a; hooks, 1993; Thompson, 1996; Wellman, 1996). To varying degrees and in various ways, almost all of us live part of our lives in the margin(s), on the border(s) (Angus, 1990; Anzaldua, 1987; Clark, 1997; Clark & O'Donnell, 1999b; Connolly & Noumair, 1997; Giroux, 1992a; hooks, 1993; Thompson, 1996; Wellman, 1996). We may find enough of ourselves in the center to get by, and we may deny, consciously or unconsciously, the parts of ourselves condemned by the mainstream to the margin(s) in an effort to survive. Border pedagogy asserts that it is necessary to bring the marginalized, border reality to greater conscious attention because although most of us have sensed our identity(ies) being marginalized, we have never openly acknowledged it, at least not on multiple planes (race *and* ethnicity, *and* language, *and* socioeconomic class, *and* gender, *and* sexuality, *and* ability status, *and* so forth), including Arboleda (Angus, 1990; Anzaldua, 1987; Clark, 1997; Clark & O'Donnell, 1999b; Connolly & Noumair, 1997; Giroux, 1992a; hooks, 1993; Thompson, 1996; Wellman, 1996). Border pedagogy, in bringing mariginalized identity(ies) to the fore, creates, for those who reside to varying degrees and in various ways on borders, a sense of freedom, the freedom to enjoy who they are in the current moment, instead of psychologically withholding this enjoyment from themselves until a time in the future where social change work has created the context for the margins to become the center, until Eurocentric society becomes multicultural society (Angus, 1990; Anzaldua, 1987; Clark, 1997; Clark & O'Donnell, 1999b; Connolly & Noumair, 1997; Giroux, 1992a; hooks, 1993; Thompson, 1996; Wellman, 1996). Many borderlands residents feel as if they are waiting for a "revolution" to appreciate themselves, waiting for the center to reflect them, to affirm them, to affirm their experiences, their psychological, emotional, social, political, cultural and other norms (Angus, 1990; Anzaldua, 1987; Clark, 1997; Clark & O'Donnell, 1999b; Connolly & Noumair, 1997; Giroux, 1992a; hooks, 1993; Thompson, 1996; Wellman, 1996). This is not to suggest that they expect nor actually want this to become a concrete reality, that they simply want to reverse the terms of the contradiction by centering the margins and marginalizing the center (Clark, 1997). On the contrary, and perhaps in some ways unfortunately and in other ways fortunately, their underlying belief is that the progressive postmodern reality lies in the continual *process* of decentering not in the finished *product* of having decentered (Angus, 1990; Anzaldua, 1987; Clark, 1997; Clark & O'Donnell, 1999a; Connolly & Noumair, 1997; Giroux, 1992a; hooks, 1993; Thompson, 1996; Wellman, 1996).

Despite in many ways having raised the status of the borderlands resident via border pedagogy, the sense of longing for centeredness often persists (Angus, 1990; Anzaldua, 1987; Clark, 1997; Clark & O'Donnell, 1999a; Connolly & Noumair, 1997; Giroux, 1992a; hooks, 1993; Thompson, 1996; Wellman, 1996). Realistically speaking, life in the margins *is* a struggle, life in a psychological, emotional, social, political, political and especially physical border community *is* a struggle (Angus, 1990; Anzaldua, 1987; Clark, 1997; Clark & O'Donnell, 1999a; Connolly & Noumair, 1997; Giroux, 1992a; hooks, 1993; Thompson, 1996; Wellman, 1996). People living in the margins *do* want their realities reflected in the mainstream, they *do* want them centered, they *do* want to rupture the Eurocentric norms that have been socially constructed against their self interest. They *do* want people who look, think, talk, walk, interact, smell, and so forth more like they do in positions of power, making decisions that will positively influence their life, their livelihood, their self-expression and that of others heretofore relegated to varying degrees and in various fashions to the margins (Angus, 1990; Anzaldua, 1987; Clark, 1997; Clark & O'Donnell, 1999a; Connolly & Noumair, 1997; Giroux, 1992a; hooks, 1993; Thompson, 1996; Wellman, 1996).

Still, the sense of freedom border pedagogy engenders can feel liberatingly unbridled. In undertaking a reanalysis of our autobiographies vis-à-vis how borders have impacted them, we must begin to think about how borders have been constructed in our lives around aspects of our identities (e.g., race, ethnicity, language, socioeconomic class), how and why we learned to observe, cross, and in some cases also eradicate those borders, and how the consciousnesses that ensued led us to other aspects of our identities (e. g., gender, sexuality, ability status; Angus, 1990; Anzaldua, 1987; Clark, 1997; Clark & O'Donnell, 1999a; Connolly & Noumair, 1997; Giroux, 1992a; hooks, 1993; Thompson, 1996; Wellman, 1996).

After looking at border issues in our autobiographies, we must begin to look for examples of border crossing in the everyday when it involves a challenge to the status quo, the center; "border crossing as liberation" (Clark, 1997). For example, a working-class Mexican American teen rediscovering herself as "Chicana" after reading, *This Bridge Called My Back: Writings By Radical Women of Color* (Moraga & Anzaldúa, 1981) rather than assimilating herself as "Hispanic" or "Spanish" after hearing Linda Chávez, former spokesperson for the English Only Movement, speak (this latter occurrence should be called "border terrorism" (Clark, 1997).

It is particularly interesting to find examples of "border crossing as liberation" in popular culture. One interesting such example emerged in the media and was discussed in the journal *Race Traitor* (Ignatiev & Garvey, 1996). The philosophical gist of this discussion, as mentioned previously, was that even White antiracists (neo-liberals) become so invested in their status as such that in the process they reify both race and Whiteness in such a way that they simply end up perpetuating, not dismantling, racism and White privilege. Hence, the only recourse for Whites genuinely committed to dismantling racism is for them to engage in the utter abolition of Whiteness altogether. In the introduction of the journal, the authors detail the circumstances of a small group of White teenagers who have taken on so-called Black identities through their attire. Whereas the teens call their association "Free To Be Me," their town refers to them as "wiggers," White niggers. The authors argue that the emergence of this conflict is a sign that the White race is beginning to disintegrate. Taken at face value this is a compelling example of border crossing as liberation. However, it could also be analyzed as border terrorism. Just because they dress "hip-hop" and appeared on a Black-hosted talk show denouncing their school for expelling them and their town for attacking their association does not mean that they did at the time nor will in the future think and act as abolitionists. They could still engage in actively racist behavior. The clothing could be an *appropriation* of Black culture in their minds, taking from Blacks for themselves, an act of colonization. Such culture crossover is not necessarily to be seen as a sign of "unwhitening," border crossing as liberation, but rather corporate marketing having the effect of increasing the level of repression in Communities Of Color. White parents, with access to institutional power based on skin color or the perception of skin color, unhappy with the Black influence in their community, put this message out, the media picks it up, and the Yusef Hawkins' story (a young Black man who was murdered for simply being in a White community[9] gets repeated over and over again (border terrorism; Clark, 1997).

Another, perhaps better, example of "border crossing as liberation" exists in the humor of Lesbian feminist comedian, Kate Clinton. In one joke, Clinton retells the story of a family gathering that she attended with her lover. After the gathering (after Clinton and her lover had left), one of her nieces, a 7 or 8 year old, asked her mother, Clinton's sister, "Can lesbians have a baby?" Her mother explained the options two women could pursue to have a child (artificial insemination, invitro fertilization, adoption, etc.) and how these differed from the main option available to heterosexual couples (intercourse). Clinton's niece reflected on this information for a moment and responded by saying, "But [Lesbians] can still try [to have a baby], right?" We can understand this to be the child's way of recognizing first, that sex is not just for reproduction but for pleasure, and second, that heterosexuals do not have a corner on the market of pleasure, both border crossing observations on her part reflecting a great deal of critical thought (Clark, 1997).

Two other interesting examples come from Nike commercials (1995a, 1995b). The first commercial challenged gender borders (Nike, 1995a). This commercial depicted several young girls citing statistics that positively correlate female self-esteem with sports involvement. For example, one girl begins a sentence with, "If you let me play sports . . . " and a second girl finishes the sentence with, "I will be more likely to leave a man who beats me."

Contrast these border crossing sentiments with the relatively recent status quo position taken by the Pope. A study on female distance runners (Women's Health Clinic, 1986) detailed their propensity to become amenorrheic (to lose their menstrual periods) due to decreased body fat; consequently, their fertility decreased as well. In a response to this study, the Pope came out against women's sports citing them as a form of birth control (Women's Health Clinic, 1986).

The second Nike commercial (1995b) shows a healthy male distance runner, running over various terrains while the text, "Ten miles a day . . . Seven days a week . . . 365 days a year . . ." appears on the screen below him. This is followed by a few seconds of no text and then the text, "HIV Positive" appears. In this commercial the border crossing messages that come to mind are, "Who is healthy?" "What does healthy look like?" "People *live* with HIV statuses, not just die from them." "What does a person with an HIV status look like?" And so forth. However, the fact that the runner in the commercial is brown skinned and his surname is Spanish (his name appears on the screen before the text runs) might lead some to the border terrorist conclusion, "only Latinas and Latinos have HIV."

A particularly excellent example of border crossing in popular culture is embodied in the heart and soul of the musical rap group, *Delinquent Habits*. One of its members identifies himself as a "Blaxican," half Black and half Mexican, a perfect example of racial and linguistic border crossing. The name of one of the group's songs, "Trés Delinquentes" (Delinquent Habits, 1995) also illustrates linguistic border crossing in much the same way that many of their lyrics do by integrating Spanish, English, Pachuquismo (Chicana and Chicano "street" Spanish) and Jive (Black "street" English, a.k.a., "Ebonics"). "Delinquente" is a cross between the English word, "delinquent" and the Spanish word "delincuente." This song also illustrates the group's ability to cross borders musically, combining multilingual and multidialectical raps with beat boxing, hip hop, and mixed in pieces from the original score of, "The Lonely Bull," an instrumental ballad indigenous to Spain but adopted, especially with Mariachi trumpeting, by México (Alpert, 1995). The group's lyrics speak to border crossing as well, detailing their struggle as boys becoming men to define themselves in a society that relegates them to the margins as less than men. "One Blaxican . . . sittin' hard like an Aztec, swift like a Zulu, this is how I kick it when I'm speakin' to my gente. Trés Delinquentes, step into the madness."

Living in the borderlands, having to "border walk," negotiate between the margin(s) and center, on a daily basis one is constantly reminded by mass media how far one's circumstances deviate from the norm, the mainstream, the "center," in terms of racial and ethnic culture, language, socioeconomic class status, religious or spiritual affiliation, generational culture, size and appearance culture, geography, topography, and climate, social codes, and on and on and on. (Ehrlich, 1994; Media Educational Foundation, 1996).

Arboleda recounts many border life, border walking experiences in *In the Shadow of Race*. For example, in chapter 19, he longs for anonymity, a place where he can go and no one will look at him because he is not "their kind," or in an effort to figure out "what" he is. Ironically, despite being a performer, one who tells his autobiography, he longs for the opportunity to get off the borderlands stage, at least when he is not actually performing, intending to perform; when he is simply out in public he wants to be able to "blend." Like other People of Color(s), who are visually perceived to be "Other" to some degree, in some way, Arboleda longs to not have to preoccupy himself with being exceptional when in public, particularly neat and clean, extraordinarily well-mannered, and so forth, because he is seen as a "representative" of his group (whatever group that may be) as opposed to simply an individual. If he goes out casually or sloppily, is aloof or downright rude, he reinforces the stereotype that *all* People of Color are messy and dirty, arrogant and aggressive (Delgado, 1995). When a White person does exactly the same thing, they are simply viewed as an unkempt and/or obnoxious individual, and not as but one more example of the inferiority of their "group" (Delgado, 1995).

Arboleda also recounts having to negotiate different customs, those normative for him (an eclectic mix from his multiple experiences but ultimately converging to some degree on generally Asian and more specifically Japanese ones) and the Eurocentric customs around which life is structured in the United States (chaps. 14 through 18). And, Arboleda discusses how being a borderlands resident negatively impacts the freedom with which he may travel and the differentially greater degree to which he is policed (chap. 19).

Perhaps most compelling is the border walking that border tenants must engage in to maintain relationships with more mainstream landladies and lords so to speak (Angus, 1990; Anzaldua, 1987; Clark, 1997; Clark & O'Donnell, 1999a; Connolly & Noumair, 1997; Giroux, 1992a; hooks, 1993; Thompson, 1996; Wellman, 1996). An excellent example of this exists in the story Arboleda relates in chapter 16 about his and his friend Vonni's (a Black woman) trip to their White friend's New Hampshire home during a holiday break from college. Initially, the visit reawakens Arboleda's desire for his mother, father, brother, and he to come back together as a family. But this thought is interrupted when he overhears the White friend's father use the term "nigger." He says nothing but is full of despair the rest of the day. In the evening, Vonni comes into the room where he is staying and addresses the use of the term with Arboleda. She identifies that the comment also made her feel full of despair but that both she and him would just have to let it go to maintain their friendship with the White woman and, more generally, they would have to let similar things go in the future if they were going to get through life more or less successfully.

Herein lays a quintessential border walking contradiction, to maintain friendships, relationships, employment, and so forth, within the mainstream, marginalized people have to ignore or "eat" racism and other forms of discrimination (Angus, 1990; Anzaldua, 1987; Clark, 1997; Clark & O'Donnell, 1999a; Connolly & Noumair, 1997; Giroux, 1992a; hooks, 1993; Thompson, 1996; Wellman, 1996). If they react, they are seen as the antagonists. The act of discrimination to which they are reacting is not only not viewed as antagonistic, it is often altogether denied as in, "you must be mistaken" or "that is not what was said, you misunderstood," or it is characterized as "not meant that way" or "not that big a deal," trivialized (as previously discussed with respect to racial power dynamics earlier). The initial act of discrimination is denied or made benign because it is an act congruous with the institutionalized norms of society (Jackson, 1976a, 1976b; Jackson & Hardiman, 1988). The reaction to the act is characterized as antagonistic precisely because it calls those norms into question (Jackson, 1976a, 1976b; Jackson & Hardiman, 1988). In so doing, it carries with it the possibility of revealing that those norms are not only not neutral but that they preserve a status quo, afford privilege to some based on group membership while taking it from others for parallel reasons (Laing & Cooper, 1971; Loewen, 1995; Novick, 1995; Oakes, 1985; Powell, 1996; Seldon, 1992; Spring, 1997; Takaki, 1993; Zinn, 1970, 1980). The reaction threatens the illusion of a just, fair, and equitable society. If the reaction is heeded the status quo position of absolute power is ever-so-slightly eroded, made potentially more relative, and that is a threat to the status quo's way of life (Laing & Cooper, 1971; Loewen, 1995; Novick, 1995; Oakes, 1985; Powell, 1996; Seldon, 1992; Spring, 1997; Takaki, 1993; Zinn, 1970, 1980).

This speaks to the differential impact of discrimination, in this case racism, on the centered and the marginalized. Although members of both groups' experiences are effected psychologically and physically by it, the impacts and their respective costs are divergent (Kovel, 1984; Laing & Cooper, 1971; Tatum, 1987, 1997; Thoman & Sillen, 1972).

Psychologically, People of Color describe having to live in a "schizophrenic" world, a world or rather worlds in which they must adeptly function with respect to more than one reality; the realities they know in the context of their own experience in the majority White culture (realities of which most Whites are unaware), and the contradictory reality constructed by the ideology of White supremacy and in the context of which most Whites function unidimensionally (Laing & Cooper, 1971; Loewen, 1995; Novick, 1995; Oakes, 1985; Powell, 1996; Seldon, 1992; Spring, 1997; Takaki, 1993; Zinn, 1970, 1980). This second reality negates the validity of the first, it is *the* modern reality whereas the former is *a* postmodern one. Living in postmodern realities, People of Color are forced to deal with dualities and multiplicities, what they know to be true from their own experiences (the floor tile is blue), and conversely, inversely, and so forth, what White people (what the ideology of White supremacy, while simultaneously responsible for constructing the racist context for those experiences and operating in a fashion divorced from those experiences) tells them is true, tells them is their experience (the floor tile is green; Laing & Cooper, 1971; Loewen, 1995; Novick, 1995; Oakes, 1985; Powell, 1996; Seldon, 1992; Spring, 1997; Takaki, 1993; Zinn, 1970, 1980).

Most White people, functioning in the modern reality, do not come to experience these dualities or multiplicities, instead they live their everyday monodimensionally, as if their experiences were everyone's (Hardiman, 1979, 1982; Helms, 1990a, 1990b, 1995). But, there are at least dualities if not multiplicities for some White people according to Dennis (1981). Unfortunately, they are usually socialized to deny them at a very early age. Dennis (1981) describes this phenomenon, which he relates occurring most commonly in the experiences of children raised in the "old" south, as a "double psycho-social consciousness."

This consciousness emerges when a White child reaches about 5 years of age, the time when their parents begin to forcibly socialize them into conscious racism; when they are no longer allowed to play with the Black children in the community, who they have known and loved all of their short lives; when they are told, in various and sundry ways, that Black people are "bad" and White people are "good" and so they must now have significant interactions with only Whites. This puts the White child in the precarious position of having to construct their racial identity in a manner congruent with their own, organic experiences of Blacks as friends and therefore positive, or in a manner congruent with their parents' expectations that Blacks are not friends and therefore negative. The White child, at the mercy of their parents for survival, has little chance of escaping the institutionalized racism with which they are being indoctrinated. Although some White children (like Children and Adults of Color) learn to live with the duality, the double psycho-social consciousness, what they know to be true (the floor tile is blue), and what they have to tell their parents they believe is true (the floor tile is green), most White children learn to abandon their organic truth, to eradicate it from their memories, and adopt the socially constructed truth of their parents.

Whites confronted, via interracial friendships or relationships, via living in physical border communities, and so forth, with the dualities and multiplicities inherent in border life, can begin to either relearn or learn for the first time to see and acknowledge these dualities and multiplicities (Hardiman, 1979, 1982; Helms, 1990a, 1990b, 1995). However, because they are often marginalized by their own community for doing such, many retreat from border experiences or experiences that force the confrontation of the realities of borders (Hardiman, 1979, 1982; Helms, 1990a, 1990b, 1995). Once again, Whites (like People of Color) are forced to deny their organic reality (the floor tile is blue), in favor of the socially constructed one (the floor tile is green), if they want to continue to enjoy all the benefits of White privilege (McIntosh, 1989, 1992).

It is in this manner that the ideology of White supremacy is constructed and perpetuated (Haney López, 1996). And beyond these psychological costs to People of Color (and Whites) perpetrated by this ideology, there are physical ones as well. People of Color, especially Blacks, suffer in much greater measure from stress and high blood pressure, and have shorter life expectancies than Whites (Sue & Sue, 1990)[10]. Although many suggest that these differences are simply a function of lifestyle "choices" (diet, exercise, and so forth), they forget that lifestyle "choices" are predicated on the system of privilege (White supremacy) that affords Whites greater access to education, employment, decent housing, decent healthcare, and the like (Giroux, 1977, 1993, 1996, 1997; McLaren, 1995).

Racial borderlands are riddled with hidden abysses. Negotiating around these abysses successfully (surviving them both psychologically and physically) is a daunting task. Racial borderlands are also graced with incredibly fertile terrain; spaces where new ways of being, knowing, and acting take root, emerge, grow, and even flourish despite the tremendous forces operating to prevent this. Arboleda's being, knowing, and acting to bring about social justice for all is a testament to all that is negative, positive, negative and positive, and neither negative nor positive about these borderlands; what is simply the borderlands.

NOTES

[1]"Reification" can be understood as the taking of an abstract idea or concept and treating it as if it were a concrete reality.

[2]"Cosmology" can be understood as an intuitive way of knowing, organic knowledge, and/or knowledge gained from subconscious or even unconscious experience.

[3]Frances Cress Welsing, a noted psychologist postulates that the seeming obsession of Whites with their own superiority and the inferiority of People of Color, especially Blacks, is but an inversion of the truth. In fact, she argues, White people are really proccupied with their own inferiority, their inability to produce skin pigmentation. In an effort to escape the sense of inferiority that comes from this inability, they project negative characterizations onto those who can do what they cannot, in essence demonizing "Others" for "flaunting" the ability to produce pigment. By inference, this raises the status of Whites. At the same time, Welsing points out, Whites flock to beaches to tan themselves despite the very real risks of skin cancer, and have babies with People of Color so that they can lay claim to having produced something (offspring) with pigmentation (1970).

[4]Certainly, the Black Identity Devlelopment model (and even the White one to a lesser degree) could be expanded to address second language issues related to the debate regarding Black English (a.k.a., Ebonics).

[5]Certainly all of the other models could be expanded to address issues of spirituality as is appropriate as well.

[6]This short-coming also suggests that new conceptualizations of racial identity development and, more generally, identity development, need to be articulated to extend to those with more global life experiences (Rattansi, 1994).

[7]Referring back to the White Identity Development model, White people are limited by other White people, by the ideology of White supremacy, in defining themselves as White when they become active antiracists (Active Resistance; Hardiman, 1979, 1982), See Clark & O'Donnell, 1999a.

[8]We should remember that 50% of all marriages "fail" or end (not to mention the statistics on committed relationships) whether the partners are of the same or different races (The Education vs. Incarceration Clearinghouse, 1998).

[9]It should be noted that this young man went into this community to purchase a car; he was beat up because community residents made the incredibly racist assumption that he was there to meet a White girlfriend (Miller, 1996).

[10]Interestingly, Blacks who survive into their eighties have the longest life expectancy of all groups.

4

Critique and Problematization of Voice in *In the Shadow of Race*

Arboleda's story is full of contradictions, and clearly, contradictions are the essence of all human existence (Dussell, 1993; McGowan, 1991; Rattansi, 1994; Rosaldo, 1993; Smart, 1992; Young, 1990). However, it is important to critique and problematize Arboleda's perspectives in the context of these contradictions to broaden the effectiveness of using his experience to explore the endless complexities of race and racial discrimination beyond what even he himself could imagine. This is to say that what Arboleda offers us unconsciously, as a person "in process" within the autobiography and continuing today, is as rich and valuable a learning reference as what he offers us consciously, as a person who has gone through the experiences he details having learned this, that, and so forth, from them. We can learn from his unfinishedness, his unrecognized or at least uncontested prejudices, his unrealized or unacknowledged competing interests. It is important to remember that this is the case for all of us. We all have these contradictions, what we know about ourselves and what we still have to know, although really may never. This is, hopefully, what reminds us to be humble. Arboleda's humility in putting his whole contradictory self into, ironically, black and white for us to read, analyze, critique, and problematize should be taken as a living example of what we all must be willing to do, reveal ourselves, if we are ever to come together as honestly committed to creating a better place for everyone to be all of who they are.

In chapter 1, Arboleda states, "In the next 20 years, the average American will no longer be technically White. This will have to be represented in the media, in the workplace, and in the schools, not out of charitable interest, but out of necessity" (p. 5). In chapter 17, he echoes this statement in asking, "How could America, Hollywood, or Disney, in their self-proclaimed 'innocence,' manage to elude that truth [the multicultural reality] for so long, and how long could the charade last?" (p. 163). Unfortunately, we have only to look to the recent past in South Africa to know that a numerical minority population that is in command of all of the economic and political power in a nation *has* to represent no one but themselves and can ignore everyone else for a very long time (Mandela, 1990). One can appreciate Arboleda's earnest hope that it be otherwise, but even profoundly earnest hope does not make for reality. The reality is born, again looking to South Africa as an example, of revolutionary action by those seeking representation and voice. To effect this reality, all of us must engage in some form of struggle to engender change (Mandela, 1990).

Arboleda recognizes the importance of such struggle in some contexts but fails to acknowledge it, or shies away from acknowledging it in others. For example, in chapters 21, 22, and 24, Arboleda talks about lobbying for a multicultural category as one step on the road to eradicating racial categorization altogether. However, in chapter 20, he takes a decidedly anti-union position, characterizing union laborers as "lazy" and "inefficient" among other things. The reader is left with the impression that Arboleda has no idea of how highly parallel the labor union struggle is with his own. What Arboleda characterizes as "lazy" and "inefficient" is more aptly characterized as an act of survival or resistance, slowing work down to draw it out and guarantee a paycheck over a longer period of time or slowing work down as a passive aggressive form of protest against unjust working conditions, respectively. One could characterize Arboleda's decision to send out a résumé with his name spelled more "Italian" as an act of assimilation, an act of selling out his cultural background, or as an act of survival, a clever way to manipulate a racist system stacked against him to his favor (chap. 19). The characterization offered all depends on what consciousness is attributed to both the union laborers and Arboleda.

In chapter 26, we find Arboleda guilty of oversimplifying racial dynamics, again perhaps the function of his lack of knowledge. In one foul swoop, Arboleda dismisses 20 years of advocacy by the Association of Black Psychologists in favor of same race adoption (see Part III). Both same race and cross-race adoption have pros and cons. There is no easy answer. Is a child better off in a loving home regardless of race than being forever moved from foster home to foster home? Absolutely. Is a Child of Color psychologically better off in the loving home of adoptive parents that are from her or his same cultural background? Absolutely. Can a loving White family adequately prepare a Child of Color or Colors to survive in a racist society? That is a much harder question to answer. Maybe. It depends on the White family, their support network (i.e., do they have Of Color family members and/or friends, or affiliations with an organization like a church or community center in which People of Color comprise significant percentages and have the ability to make meaningful contributions?), what kind of training and education the adoption agency provides for them, and so forth (Bennett, 1986; Katz, 1978; Manning, 1995; Tatum, 1987). Arboleda falls into the trap of substituting his opinion for knowledge, something everyone does and something everyone must learn to stop doing. We must open ourselves up to hear what we may not want to hear. Clearly, as Arboleda admits from the outset (preface & chap. 1), he is jealous that anyone can have a "cultural home," be with a community of like people, when he has only one other person with whom he shares that bond, his brother, and with whom the relationship is admittedly, from his perspective, contentious. It is almost as if Arboleda wants us all to be islands so that he will have a peer group. He needs to recognize that his peer group will emerge when he accepts that other "Others" will define themselves differently from he and yet will still likely accept him if he accepts them.

Arboleda also fluctuates in terms of challenging discrimination in one instance and not in others. For example, in chapter 7, he makes a point of the "White flight" occurring in his paternal grandmother's and grandfather's neighborhood in Parkway Village, New York but fails to characterize his own "White flight" from Jamaica Plain to Sommersville, Massachusetts (chap. 20). Nor does he problematize in a significant enough way, his own class privilege in being able to take flight, relocate, when others cannot. An interesting analysis can be made of the tortured irony in that at the same time that three generations of Arboleda's family are being terrorized by racial and ethnic discrimination everywhere they go, they are enjoying relatively significant class privilege. Imagine the comparative struggle for those who face the same racial and ethnic discrimination but lack the means to even partially mitigate it with class access.

Arboleda argues that because all cultures are unique they cannot be critiqued, interfered with, or challenged. And then he does just that as the ensuing discussion illustrates. However, that he does this may not be such a bad thing. Certainly, it is important to respect the uniqueness and sanctity of all cultures. However, nothing is above critique or challenge, and cultural interference can occur, depending on how one defines it, simply when a cultural outsider, no matter how cross-culturally respectful, interacts with insiders. Cultural critique and challenge can be done from the bane of ethnocentrism or the spirit of global liberation. Certainly there are good and bad aspects of every culture. For example, oppression of women is manifest in some way in every culture: "witch" burning, foot binding, genital mutilation, domestic violence, rape, and so forth (Bhachu, 1996; Davis, 1981; DuBois & Rúiz, 1990; Frankenberg, 1993a; Freidman, 1995; Griffin, 1995; Kuhn & Wolpe, 1978; Lorde, 1984; Rich, 1979; Ware, 1992). Simply because the way this oppression is manifest is unique to each culture and simply because in so being it is culturally sanctioned, does not mean it is okay. On the contrary, from a sociopolitically conceptualized multicultural perspective this oppression must not only be critiqued and challenged but aggressively interfered with until it stops. Arboleda's critique and challenge of all cultures to accept him, his interference in those cultures by being who he is in them, is necessary.

In chapters 12, 14, and 15, Arboleda talks about how the Japanese sanction racist behavior but then he fails to make the parallel reference to the United States, Germany, and so forth. He also asks, again in reference to Japan, how a person is supposed to immerse her or himself in a culture that does not accept outsiders, but once again, fails to make the parallel with the United States, Germany, and so on. In a third instance, in chapter 14, he makes a big deal of detailing his mother's inability to cope in Japan because of how isolated and discriminated against she was there, affirming her in this isolation. Yet, he does not make as correspondingly a big deal of his paternal grandmother's, paternal grandfather's, father's, brother's, and even his own inability to cope in the Phillipines, the United States, Germany, and Japan, more or less respectively, because of how isolated and discriminated against they all were and continue to be (save his grandfather). In this way, Arboleda tacitly assigns greater value to his mother's negative experience than he does even his own, a function of his having internalized racism (Freire, 1970). Although there are parallels in all of these experiences of isolation and discrimination, his mother's reality as a White woman is different than the reality everyone else mentioned faces; even in being the object of isolation and discrimination, she still enjoys great privilege based on skin color (Feagin & Vera, 1995; Terry, 1975). This is another example or how Arboleda often fails to challenge his assimilation to discriminatory norms. This assimilation can also be seen in his failure to contest his mother's "jungle fever," her making exotic of darker skinned people, her attempts to darken herself, all without respect to the sociopolitical reality of racism (Welsing, 1970). How bourgeois she is to idolize darkness while enjoying White skin privilege. In one other instance, in chapter 20, Arboleda describes having learned to avoid "certain dangerous neighborhoods." Despite this he is still mugged (chap. 21). To his credit, he does not use the mugging as an excuse to fuel the racist attitudes expressed by the police officer showing him the mug shots. But, in chapter 19, when he overhears a Japanese family referring to non-Japanese as "gaijin" in the United States, he does use his experience of having been sort of emotionally mugged as forever "gaijin" in Japan as an excuse to engage in a retaliatorily racist act toward them.

Clearly, these four examples illustrate Arboleda's profound angst in feeling culturally more Japanese than anything else and feeling more "at home" in Japan than anywhere else, and yet not being affirmed in either feeling by Japanese people, even life-long Japanese friends. This dynamic has taken its toll on Arboleda. Beginning in chapter 12 and continuing through many subsequent chapters, we see just how much Arboleda yearns to belong in Japan. His willingness to, even if reluctantly, collude in the sexist behavior of the store clerk owner to earn only the back-handed compliment "Teja, you might be Japanese after all!" speaks volumes (p. 107). It is also reminiscent of a virtually identical compensatory acceptance strategy used by another "multiethnic, multicultural, 'multiracial' American," Tiger Woods. In being so rejected in the sport he promises to redefine because of his skin color, Tiger Woods began telling outrageously sexist jokes, seemingly to earn entrée with golf colleagues as "one of the guys," presumably attempting to redraw the insider/outsider lines along gender instead of race (McCormick & Begley, 1996; Reilly, 1996). This is but one more of the ways in which the institutionalized nature of discrimination across the various social membership groups encourages targets of each form of discrimination to play each other against the middle so to speak, jockeying for relative or compartmentalized access, one rung above the more "Otherized" "Other" (Freire, 1970). In the end, Arboleda affirms himself as profeminist and a committed antisexist man. It is important to recognize his struggle to accomplish this: beginning with the comment, even if made in jest, about a "Miss Multiracial American" contest in the preface; to his being an auditory witness of domestic violence but doing *nothing*, not even calling 911 to try and stop it in chapter 19; to his affirmation of men needing to cry and needing to be comforted in so doing by other men without it calling their gender or sexuality into question, at the same time without it conveying homophobia in chapter 17; to his ardently stated resolution to change the world by challenging racism *and* sexism—giving them equal status—in the media in chapters 20 and 22.

In chapter 20, Arboleda warns of the consequences of "cultural trespassing" (p. 204). Yet, during his cross-country odyssey of the United States, he experiments with his racial identity by not shaving, showering, and tanning in an effort to tempt people to "react" to him. He problematizes his behavior by questioning why he would self-identify to encourage increased discrimination, but he does not talk about the luxury he enjoys in being able to "go back," to shave, shower, and avoid the sun, nor does he consider the impact of his actions in this regard on others. If, as he suggests, in doing this experiment, he is perceived by Whites as Mexican, what is the cost of his behavior to real Mexicans? Increased police repression? Increased antibilingual education sentiment? And, is his behavior in this instance not an act of cultural trespassing? Students need to explore these and other such questions in the discussion of this chapter.

This leads to another concern. Arboleda often begins a critical analysis of his experiences but stops short of completing it, leaving the reader only part way along on the journey he started them out on. For example, in chapter 18, Arboleda relates the contradiction he feels in crashing an all White dentist's reception at a hotel and then in seeing all Blacks standing in an unemployment line just outside the hotel. His analysis consists of his feeling guilty about being dressed up and wanting to change into casual clothes. As if somehow this would convey his solidarity with the Blacks? With their poverty? Or as if this would erase or at least hide his relative privilege? Because Arboleda's struggle for acceptance as a culturally "mixed" person is so persistent, pervasive, and seemingly permanent (Bell, 1992), he seems to have trouble recognizing that despite this struggle, he is still privileged. And this privilege is not just in terms of gender, class, educational level, and so forth, but even in terms of skin color. Despite having the sense of belonging essentially nowhere, of having no "cultural home," he is afforded incrementally greater access to participation in society than darker skinned people are (Haizlip, 1994). And although many darker skinned people may have a greater sense of belonging somewhere, may have a "cultural home," they bear the brunt of racial discrimination, and staying out of the sun does not mitigate it (Delgado, 1995). Arboleda resists acknowledging this. In fact, everyone does; we all have a hard time acknowledging that with all of our troubles, anyone could have it worse, and yet, someone always does (Nieto, 1998). But, just because someone else may have it worse does not mean that we do not struggle; it need not mitigate our struggle. However, it does require us to recognize the way different forms of oppression are manifest differently and how multiple forms of oppression compound each manifestation exponentially (Adams, Bell, & Griffin, 1997).

Related to this, in chapter 20, Arboleda makes what is perhaps the most arrogant proclamation that "no one" can understand what he is going through, not even his friend Ukumbra (p. 200). Again, this speaks volumes about his lack of knowledge; in this case his knowledge deficit has to do with Black history and experience in the United States (Kunjufu, 1995; Takaki, 1993). Here again, Arboleda characterizes his struggle as the worst, unprecedented. He must come to understand that although his struggle is different from that of other people, they can relate to it if he will let them and if, in turn, he accepts their struggle as just as unique; he must also own his privilege relative to his struggle (Adams, Bell, & Griffin, 1997).

Arboleda's ability to access showers in college and university gymnasiums while homeless (detailed in chap. 19), is another example of the duality of his struggle and privilege. Many people would not have this access either because of a lack of knowledge about the ease with which one might be able to use such a facility, or, because skin color or other more "severe" physical attribute or diminished psychological or developmental capacity would, despite their knowledge of such facilities, arouse suspicions in others such that they would be barred from using the facilities at the outset. That is, because of their appearance and/or behavior, students would be inclined to think that they did not belong in the facilities and call campus security to have them removed.

One more example of this duality is a more complicated one. This example is in reference to Arboleda's relationship with his friend Ukumbra. In chapter 14, Arboleda details a series of events involving classmates of his in Japan, who are either part Japanese or like him otherwise "mixed." In an attempt to claim Japan as their home, Japanese culture as their own, in essence to proclaim themselves Japanese, this group of students try and impose Japanese relational hierarchy on each other to try and "prove" their Japaneseness. The pain they feel in not being "all" Japanese, and/or in not being accepted as Japanese is manifest in the negative versus positive way they reproduce this tradition, through force using violence versus through honor using respect. Arboleda is able to understand how meaningful this struggle is for his classmates despite how erroneously conceived, he still gives it value, he affirms it. Arboleda wants this "cultural home" as much as his classmates do, he just rejects their means of trying to acquire it. Perhaps he recognizes, at least for himself, its fruitlessness, though he is cautious not to suggest that it will be equally fruitless for any of them. He affords them the opportunity to define "home" as they need to.

However, when Arboleda's friend Ukumbra embarks on a parallel journey to claim a homeland, culture, and identity for himself, Arboleda challenges the integrity of his journey (chaps. 22 & 26). For Arboleda, being something by heritage does not entitle one to the associated culture, yet, not being something by heritage does not preclude one from entitlement to the associated culture. Arboleda argues that being of African heritage does not entitle Ukumbra to claim an African cultural identity because he was not socialized African. Yet, Arboleda rejects the Japanese position that if he is not Japanese by heritage, despite being socialized Japanese, he cannot be culturally Japanese. Implied in Arboleda's argument is somehow the rule that culture has to be socialized from birth or shortly thereafter and cannot be something to which an adult chooses to socialize her or himself. Ironically, Arboleda goes on to suggest that Ukumbra also cannot become culturally African because culture cannot be communicated through biology. And yet, Arboleda and his brother, neither of whom were socialized to be overridingly Filipino, experience the traditional Filipino "breeze," the visit by their paternal grandfather's spirit on his death (chap. 25). Arboleda did not have to know of this cultural norm to experience it. Perhaps culture found another way? Through his soul? Ultimately, all of us need to allow others to define themselves in whatever way liberates them from racism and other forms of discrimination.

One last issue that needs to be addressed here is Arboleda's word choice, as alluded to in chapter 2 of this guide. One simply confusing word choice of Arboleda's is that at different times he uses the same term *"Indian"* to describe two different groups, both Native Americans or American Indians (people indigenous to the Americas) and South Asians (also geographically erroneously referred to as *"East Indians,"* people indigenous to India). The reader may have to reflect a bit to figure out to which group of people he is referring in each instance the term is used. As discussed in chapter 2 of this guide, words are conveyors of consciousness, which is why words and/or word choices change, to convey new consciousnesses. Native American and South Asian are both considered the more contemporary and liberatory terms for the populations being referenced in both regards here. Again, this does not mean that people from either of these groups will necessarily use these terms to describe themselves, but, it is most important for cultural outsiders to at least try and convey a contemporary and liberatory consciousness out of respect.

Arboleda also uses the term *"Gypsy"* (from whence the connotation of "gyping" someone out of something derives) another outdated and derogatory term to describe a group of people more contemporarily and liberatorily referred to as the Romany. "Gypsy" has perhaps the most confusing dictionary definition ever recorded. It is worth quoting here as it lends further credence to Arboleda's contention that race, ethnicity, and all other terms and phrases used to approximate categories of cultural identity at best fall well short of doing anything of the sort. "Gypsy . . . thought to have come from Egypt; a member of a wandering Caucasoid people with dark skin and black hair found throughout the world and believed to have originated in India" (Neufeldt & Guralnik, 1997, p. 603). This just has to be one of the most amazing examples of contradictory characterizations of a people ever: "Caucasoid" people from both Egypt and India with dark skin and black hair.

Arboleda also uses the terms *"non-White"* and *"minority,"* also mentioned in chapter 2 of this guide, to reference all People of Color. Again, these terms are problematic: "non-White" because it describes people in reference to what they are not instead of what they are, and "minority" because it references people in a diminished capacity, "minor," "less than." Although the term *People of Color* is contested, again as mentioned in chapter 2 of this guide, it is considered the most contemporary and liberatory collective reference for Native Americans or American Indians, Blacks, Asians, and Latinas and Latinos to date and, despite critiques of it, is generally more well-received than either "non-White" or "minority."

Other problematic word, term, phrase choices of Arboleda's include: *"colorful groups,"* *"Japanese flavor,"* and *"exotic mix."* These phrases perpetuate the stereotype that only People of Color are ethnic and therefore somehow more "expressive" than White people. Arboleda's use of the phrase, *"colored perceptions,"* along with multiple other light and dark imagery references throughout the text correlate positive association with lightness and negative ones with darkness. Arboleda's use of the phrases *"urban jungles"* and *"wild Indians"* reinforce stereotypes of People of Color as savages, less civilized than Whites. Given the historical reality of Blacks (to whom the "urban jungle" reference is directed given their percentages in major metropolitan areas in the United States) and Native Americans vis-à-vis Whites in the United States, these stereotypes are an example of the proclivity of those in power to reverse the truth when writing history (Daly, 1990; Welsing, 1970; see also footnote 3 in chap. 3 of this guide). This they do to characterize themselves more positively, to project onto those to whom they were savage, less civilized, the characterization of savagery and lack of civility, to literally "whitewash" the reality (Allen, 1994; Apple, 1997; Bonnett, 1996; Clark, 1999; Clark & O'Donnell, 1999a; Delgado & Stephancic, 1997; Frankenberg, 1993b; Hardiman, 1979, 1982; Helms, 1990a, 1995; Keating, 1995; Lipsitz, 1995; Nakayama & Krizek, 1995; Novick, 1995; Powell, 1996; Roediger, 1991; Shohat & Stam; 1994, Stowe, 1996; Young, 1979). Uncovering reversals of truth in our history is an educationally provocative approach to studying it. Using this critique of Arboleda as a vantage point, students could engage in analysis of historical events and their representations in educational resources and see how many other reversals they can uncover. A couple of other examples of such are: (a) the characterization of enslaved Africans as "lazy" but not the Europeans who enslaved them to work on the Europeans' behalf, and, (b) the references to women being born of men, Athena from the head of Zeus in Greek mythology and Eve from the rib of Adam in biblical history, despite the biologically limiting reality that only women are bearers of life (Daly, 1990).

Arboleda also makes multiple negative references to individuals based on body size, as "fat," "overweight," "heavy-set," as having "thighs that rub together" or "hang over" the edge of a chair, or "stomachs that hang out." Usually he makes these references about people who have in some way offended him and he almost justifies the references as fair retaliation in the manner previously described in the incident with the Japanese family (chap. 19). But at least in that case he expressed remorse. It is clear to the reader that Arboleda has unresolved prejudices regarding body size that need to be contested by readers. Related to this, he describes someone as "short but beautiful," leaving one with the impression that generally short people are not beautiful.

There is also a problem with Arboleda's reference to Immigrants of Color as "ethnic," again implying that White immigrants (and Whites in general) lack ethnicity, that they are not ethnic. This reference is also problematic because it describes the practice whereby a single family member would immigrate to the United States and subsequently try to bring the rest of the family over as only a practice that Immigrants of Color engaged in, completely omitting the mention of large numbers of White immigrants who did the same thing.

In chapter 7, Arboleda describes his sense of alienation in school as an "Other." He finds immediate kinship with a classmate who, like he, has a name considered strange by the rest of the students in the class. In a subsequent reference to this classmate's name he reflects on it and then consciously colludes (as previously discussed with respect to his colluding in the objectification of women with the Japanese store owner) in making her the "Other," more "Other" than he, by deciding that, in point of fact, as if it were a forgone conclusion, an absolute truth, her name is strange, and therefore humorous.

These words, terms, phrases are all problematic in that they perpetuate discriminatory characterizations, stereotypes, of certain groups and thereby foster instead of interrupt the prejudice and discrimination experienced by members of these groups. The overriding purpose of Arboleda's text is to challenge and eradicate discrimination. Unfortunately, even the most multiculturally evolved individual or resource is imperfect, in process, still evolving.

In closing, we must return to Arboleda's humility in putting himself out, risking the inevitability of both constructive and hostile criticism of not only his ideas and perceptions, but of his experiences as well. We must support not just his successes in, but also his attempts at liberating himself, and through him "Others," from acceptance of limiting cultural categories and identities. We must remember that there are no role models for how to be multiethnic, multicultural, multiracial, hence, Arboleda is literally "making the road by walking it" (Bell, Gaventa, & Peters, 1990), and what an important road it is.

PART II

Using
In the Shadow of Race
in Courses

5

Implications of
In the Shadow of Race
for Multicultural Education

Multicultural education is a process of comprehensive school reform and basic education for all students. It challenges and rejects racism and other forms of discrimination in schools and society and accepts and affirms the pluralism (ethnic, racial, linguistic, religious, economic, and gender, among others) that students, their communities and teachers represent. Multicultural education permeates the curriculum and instructional strategies used in schools, as well as the interactions among teachers, students, and parents, and the very way that schools conceptualize the nature of teaching and learning. Because it uses critical pedagogy as its underlying philosophy and focuses on knowledge, reflection, and action (praxis) as the basis for social change, multicultural education furthers the democratic principles of social justice. (Nieto, 1996, p. 209)

Arboleda's "multiethnic, multicultural, and 'multiracial'" struggle vis-à-vis his school experiences offers numerous examples of why multicultural educational theory and practice, goals and objectives, must be well-integrated across academic subject areas/disciplines and grade levels (kindergarten through terminal degree programs). These experiences offer all educators, those just beginning the process of becoming multicultural, those already well-established as multicultural educators, and everyone in between, a plethora of multicultural teaching opportunities.

One of the major tenets of multicultural education is that learning is not necessarily intended to make one comfortable but rather should challenge one to think critically about whatever the focus of learning is. In an article entitled, "The Myth of 'Rosa Parks the Tired'" (Kohl, 1993), the author delineates how, based on the typical representations of Ms. Parks in historical texts, students are taught to think about her role in the Alabama bus boycott as a passive and inadvertent one. These texts paint her as an apolitical, apolemic historical figure;

a figure who refused to give up her seat in the front of a bus simply because she was too tired from her day's work to move to the back. Kohl points out that although Ms. Parks was indeed tired, it was not merely from a hard day's work but rather more so that she was tired of racism, particularly the institutionalized racism that legislated that she must sit in the back of a bus because of her skin color. Her decision not to relinquish her seat was a conscious and deliberate, decidedly political act of resistance against racism. This perspective is not presented in most historical texts and therefore is not taught in most classrooms, not with respect to Ms. Parks nor any other person, event, or subject.

Multicultural education argues that by reducing learning to what is considered safe, tempered, comfortable, apolitical, polemic, and so forth, not only does the learning fail to challenge students, fail to make them think critically, it is also based on a skewed or even altogether false reality (Banks, 1991, 1992, 1994a, 1994b; Bigelow, 1990; Clark, 1993a; hooks, 1993; Nieto, 1996, 1998; Oakes, 1985; Schwartz, 1993; Shor, 1992; Sleeter, 1996; Sleeter & Grant, 1991; Walsh, 1991). In being so based, such learning is not in fact apolitical and apolemic but rather politicized and polemic from a particular point of view, once again the Eurocentric perspective. As discussed throughout this guide, the Eurocentric perspective is said to reinforce as normal the values and norms of White, Anglo Saxon, native English-speaking, middle- to upper-class, heterosexual, able-bodied and at least theoretically able-minded and emotioned, Christian, usually Protestant, usually 21 to 65 year old, reasonably thin, reasonably attractive, East coast, environmentally indifferent or hostile men, as if there was no perspective in these values and norms, as if they were simply "universal," the same for everyone (Banks, 1991, 1992, 1994a, 1994b; Bigelow, 1990; Clark, 1993a; hooks, 1993; Nieto, 1996, 1998; Oakes, 1985; Schwartz, 1993; Shor, 1992; Sleeter, 1996; Sleeter & Grant, 1991; Walsh, 1991). Additionally, the characterization of such education as safe, tempered, and comfortable raises the question, safe, tempered, and comfortable for whom? For a politically conservative school committee? Perhaps. For students in the classroom? Certainly not. Such *mis*education encourages student passivity, disinterest, and nonengagement in the curriculum while fostering cross-cultural conflict outside schools (Kunjufu, 1995). Wiley (1991) found that, "Most of the students contended that fights between students of different racial groups erupt outside of school because of a lack of knowledge about each other's culture. Hostilities are exacerbated by the lack of a school environment and curriculum that fosters understanding among students of various racial groups and academic classifications" (p. A3). Elaborating on this theme one student stated his belief that, "'If you clean the school system to where it is more of a multicultural diversity in areas of learning, then the streets will start to clean up,'" (Wiley, 1991, p. A3). In an effort to respond to the conflict ". . . the students agreed to work together toward increasing communication and sensitivity between school staff and students and toward changing the school curriculum to reflect more religious and cultural diversity" (Wiley, 1991, p. A3).

Arboleda's early childhood experiences, continuing on through to his adulthood, and persisting today, of being called every negative epithet conceivable, are further testament to the fact that racism and other forms of discrimination are alive and well and not simply in the "hidden" Eurocentric curriculum, but in the hearts and minds of even very young children who have learned, from parents, siblings, peers, teachers, school culture, societal culture, and the media among other sources, how to participate in and thus perpetuate dehumanizing and otherwise oppressive masternarratives (Chasnoff & Cohen, 1996; Derman-Sparks & the ABC Taskforce, 1989). This challenges the suggestion that by putting the multicultural into Eurocentric education that what was safe, tempered, and comfortable is now political, polemic, biased. Clearly the absence of the multicultural means that the Eurocentric bias is uncontested. It is only by bringing the multicultural into the equation that education begins to become more representative of the multiplicity of perspectives that exist relative to all knowledge, thereby creating a safer, more tempered, and more comfortable learning environment for all students. That is, only in exposing the bias, the political, the polemic, through its contestation, does the classroom welcome the voice of every student (Banks, 1991, 1992, 1994a, 1994b; Bigelow, 1990; Clark, 1993a; hooks, 1993; Nieto, 1996, 1998; Oakes, 1985; Schwartz, 1993; Shor, 1992; Sleeter & Grant, 1991; Sleeter, 1996; Walsh, 1991). And it is important to stress that this is the case for *every* student, even those for whom the Eurocentric model was supposedly designed. In *Through Students' Eyes: Racism in United States' Schools* (McLean-Donaldson, 1996), the author makes the highly salient discovery that White students do not feel privileged, advantaged, and supported by teachers' racism toward Students of Color but rather embarrassed and ashamed by it. Multicultural education attempts to rectify power imbalances in society by rectifying power imbalances in the curriculum so that all students learn that they are no more nor no less important than anyone else; not in the past, today, or in the future. Relative value assigned to a person or a people based on social group membership is a function of social construction and not anything intrinsic to that person or people (Clark, 1993a).

There are many people, events, and subjects that Arboleda references, some simply in passing, others most often from a decidedly counterhegemonic point of view that educators adapting *In the Shadow of Race* may take advantage of to engender student debate and questioning in a manner consistent with multicultural education as just discussed. Some examples will help to illustrate how this can be undertaken.

In chapter 7, Arboleda details his personal experience of having been bused from one school to another in the throws of the school desegregation movement. His experience of this historical period is (as are virtually all of his other experiences) highly unique in that as a student who was something other than Black or White he was bused from a predominantly White school to a predominantly Black one where students' perceptions of him, and his perception of himself, remained largely unchanged. He describes both Black and White classmates claiming that they "knew" he was not White but "were not sure" he was Black either. Resultingly, Arboleda continued to wonder himself as to "what" he was.

Black students from predominantly Black schools bused to predominantly White schools and White students from predominantly White schools bused to predominantly Black schools experienced school desegregation very differently, they "knew," or as Arboleda might argue, they at least lived with the steadfast illusion, that they were Black or White and that where they were being bused most everyone would be different from them (Donato, 1997; Public Broadcasting Systems, 1992). This experience became definitive for them in terms of race, having to be so clearly visually different from everyone else and having to deal with the sociopolitical ramifications of what this meant in terms of how, for Blacks, they would be treated in the educational context, and how, for Whites they *perceived* they would be treated in the educational context[1] (Bowser & Hunt, 1981; Clark, Jenkins, & Stowers, in press; Dennis, 1981; Spring, 1997). For Arboleda, this was nothing new, the players changed but the experience was largely a familiar one, being "Otherized."

The defining impact of Arboleda's busing experience was in terms of socioeconomic class rather than race. He describes in detail his reaction to the changing economic landscape from the time his school bus left Parkway Village and until it arrived in Bedford-Stuyvesant. With this experience educators are presented with the opportunity to discuss a concrete historical example correlating racism and classism (Bowles & Gintis, 1977; Goldberg, 1993a; Haymes, 1995; Kozol, 1991; Wellman, 1993).

Clearly, Arboleda's history opens the door for educators to guide students in a deeper exploration of the Civil Rights Movement, school desegregation with respect to busing as well as other things, for example legislation like *Brown versus Board of Education of Topeka*, and so forth (Spring, 1997). By using his autobiography as a starting point learning is both more personal and more grounded in the sociopolitical complexities of the time. However, to make the learning on this subject more multicultural, more comprehensive, and hence more accurate, it would also be important for educators to include discussion comparing and contrasting the Civil Rights Movement of the East, which details primarily the Black struggle for civil rights, with that much less well known of the West, which details primarily the Chicana and Chicano struggle for civil rights. By comparing and contrasting the events depicted in the Public Broadcasting Systems series "Eyes on the Prize" (Public Broadcasting System, 1992) and "¡Chicano!" (Public Broadcasting System, 1994), supplementing the latter with readings from the text, *The Other Struggle for Equal Schools: Mexican Americans During the Civil Rights Era* (Donato, 1997), students will get a more complete picture of the entirety of the Civil Rights Movement in the United States at the same time developing a sense of the concept of civil rights movements in general, how and why they emerge, their impact on individuals, Peoples, and nations.

In chapter 7, Arboleda talks about the issue of having had to sing the U.S. national anthem in school. In chapter 11, he recounts a dialogue about the meanings of the colors of the U.S. flag, in particular, the characterization of white as purity.

In several places throughout the text, Arboleda makes references to darkness and lightness; in some cases these references correlate with race-related discussions and in other places they are simply part of his own literary allusion. For example, in chapter 11, as previously discussed in chapter 3 of this guide, he details his run-in with a picture bible at a public library and his confusion regarding the depictions of people from the Middle East as light skinned and with European features, save the one or two wise men, portrayed as subservient, and Judas, the traitor, who were portrayed with dark skin. Arboleda reflects on his reaction to these pictures by revealing his initial embarrassment at seeing naked White people and then contrasts this with his recollection of feeling comparatively comfortable in having seen naked People of Color in pictures of magazines like *National Geographic* or in UNICEF commercials on television.

In the *Autobiography of Malcolm X as Told to Alex Haley* (Haley, 1986), Malcolm tells the story of how his critical consciousness regarding racism is awakened. He goes to a dictionary and looks up the words "black" and "white" and compares and contrasts their given definitions. Uniformly, black is defined in negative manners, whereas white is defined in positive ones.

Taken collectively, Arboleda's dialogues in these areas, coupled with the Malcolm X exercise that students could reexecute for themselves, create a context for educators to explore with students the correlation between U.S. patriotism and racism in the United States. In a study of American values, Dean and Suchman (1964) found that racism ranked 15th. Furthermore, they and others have revealed that the more patriotically inclined, the more of a "flag waver," "love it or leave" type of individual a U.S. citizen is, the more predisposed they are to also express active racism (Dean & Suchman, 1964; Douglas, 1972; Geertz, 1973; Williams, 1970). At the conclusion of such an analysis, students could be asked to consider what they now believe to be the implications of having to sing the national anthem in school, what is in essence state-sanctioned coerced patriotism, on the proliferation of racism in schools and society as another component of the so-called "hidden" (in reality the not-so-hidden) Eurocentric curriculum.

Arboleda makes references to Christopher Columbus, World War II, and the Vietnam War. With respect to World War II, he makes the ironic but devastatingly sobering inference that his grandfathers were actually fighting in the same war against each other. He makes other inferences as to the multiplicity of ways one can view of each of these three entities depending on one's perspective of them. This is another great opportunity for educators to take advantage of; to have students look at the implications of Columbus' "Voyage to the New World," World War II, and the Vietnam War from various perspectives. Kunjufu (1995) argues that history must be taught as events that occurred with unlimited reference points for understanding their significance, impact, and so forth. The fewer reference points considered, the more skewed our perceptions of the event is, we are left with a single or only a few relative truth(s), while the more reference points considered, the closer we get to, although never actually arriving at, the absolute truth of what really occurred. An excellent supplemental resource for revisioning Columbus is Rethinking Schools' *Rethinking Columbus* (1992), which challenges students to consider Columbus alternatively as having "bumped into," "discovered," and "invaded" the Americas. Excellent supplemental resources for opening up new ways of looking at World War II and the Vietnam War may be found in Howard Zinn's, *A People History of the United States* (1980) and *The Politics of History* (1970). Arboleda himself cites his Danish grandfather's characterization of the Nazi party as "socialist," as in the "National Socialist Party," at a time when most of the rest of the world characterized the Nazi party as fascist. Arboleda also makes the ironic connection between Hitler having commissioned the Volkswagen Beetle and its subsequent social construction as the ultimate symbol of the anti-Vietnam war peace-loving counterculture hippie generation. This connection makes for an interesting segue from one war to the next.

Within all three of these historical references also lays the opportunity to address the tenet of "manifest destiny." Excellent supplemental resources for this discussion include Ronald Takaki's, *A Different Mirror: A Multicultural History of America* (1993) and Jay Loewen's, *Lies My Teacher Told Me: Everything Your American History Textbook Got Wrong* (1995). Arboleda also makes numerous more contemporary references to a variety of things, again throughout the text, that could further the discussion of manifest destiny in a more modern-day context, sort of in the vein of "manifest destiny is alive and well and living in your backyard." For example, in chapter 15 he laments the proliferation of fast food restaurants like Kentucky Fried Chicken and McDonald's in downtown Tokyo and (a) the ensuing negative impact on Japanese people's physical health and well-being in bringing a high fat, high cholesterol diet to a country where previously, health problems related with such a diet were almost nonexistent, and, (b) the correlating erosion of Japanese people's mental well-being by encouraging people to abandon salubrious cultural traditions, in this case diet-related ones, in the quest to be more "American." The manifest destiny of the 21st century is enabled by global capitalism, territorial conquest and acquisition via psychological colonization (Guiner, 1994; Stephancic & Delgado, 1996). It uses mass marketing and media to convince people that what is culturally normative, from nature, and inarguably "better" for them, what has thousands of years of history and tradition behind it, should be voluntarily abandoned in favor of that which is culturally vacuous, virtually entirely synthetic, inarguably absolutely horrible for them, and which has no history and no tradition supporting save the almighty U.S. dollar (Guiner, 1994; Stephancic & Delgado, 1996).

Arboleda mentions Bob Hope, Al Franken, Don Rickles, Bugs Bunny, Aladdin, John Wayne, and "bleeding" Jesus in contexts that challenge their typically positive and welcome representation in the mass media. Bob Hope, Al Franken, Don Rickles, Bugs Bunny, and John Wayne he reveals as racist. Although the character Aladdin himself is not, at least overtly, racist, Arboleda reveals the racism implied in, as with the picture bible, depicting a Middle Eastern person as light skinned (Novick, 1995).

The "bleeding" Jesus commentary is perhaps the most controversial. Arboleda problematizes the impact of having an almost life-sized sculpture of a man nailed to a cross and bleeding profusely on the hearts and minds of very young children, especially those like he, not socialized Catholic and therefore presumably not even at least superficially able (as first graders) to understand its intended religious significance.

An analysis of messages and images in the public domain and/or in the mass media in terms of how they perpetuate violence, broadly conceptualized as racist, sexist, homophobic, and so forth, could follow from a discussion of Arboleda's aforementioned references. In this way, students begin to recognize the impact mass marketing and media have in influencing and even shaping individual values and belief and can dialogue about ways to interrupt and eventually eradicate this impact and/or replace it with messages and images that promote multiculturalism as positive (Media Educational Foundation, 1996; Sleeter, 1996; Sneed, 1994; Schwartz, 1993). For instance, students could write letters to television networks deconstructing as negative and expressing disdain for the discriminatory messages and imagery they identified. They could even develop positive counter messages and imagery and submit these with their letters as examples of what could be depicted instead. Connecting learning to activism is another important tenet of multicultural education. Excellent supplemental resources for developing learning in this manner can be found in the *Anti-Bias Curriculum* (Derman-Sparks & the ABC Taskforce, 1989) and in Christine Sleeter's, *Multicultural Education as Social Activism* (1996).

In addition to the messages and imagery portrayed in the media, Arboleda also references events in the news and problematizes how they are reported. In particular, Arboleda mentions the Rodney King beating and the Oklahoma City bombing. Here again, he reveals the racism in how these events were reported, the beating in terms of the use of "justifiable force" by the umpteen police officers involved but who were supposedly "threatened" by one stumbling-drunk Black man, and the bombing in terms of the references to "three Middle Eastern 'looking' men" who were supposed to have been seen, "running from the scene" (Batts, 1989; Clark & Jenkins, 1994; Ehrlich, 1994; Goldberg, 1993a; hooks, 1995; Media Educational Foundation, 1996; Seldon, 1992, Sleeter, 1996; Sneed, 1994). Discussion of these and other events could be structured around a news research project. Students could begin the project by comparing and contrasting the presentation of news events on the three television network's news with that on Black Entertainment Television's news. Furthermore, they could research the number of news sources from which all news reports derive in the United States (there are only twelve; Media Educational Foundation, 1996). They could continue by researching who owns television, radio, and Internet networks, and discuss how who owns them might influence how news is filtered before the general public hears it. An exploration of Bill Cosby's blocked attempt to purchase one of the television networks could augment this discussion (Media Educational Foundation, 1996). Students could then experiment with different ways to present news given certain information about real and/or fictitious events and discuss the factors influencing their decisions to present it whichever way they did (i.e., their own race or gender or the race or gender of the person in the news story, the geographic location of a news story, and so forth). This discussion could also include how presidential administrations use the media to market foreign and domestic policy to the U.S. public (Goldberg, 1993a; Stephancic & Delgado, 1996). Arboleda's reference in chapter 24 to the Bush administration's marketing of foreign policy with respect to Eastern Europe would make a good starting point for such discussion.

Clearly, by opening up student debate and questioning on the many issues Arboleda raises from provocatively antiracist and otherwise antidiscriminatory points of reference will make for engaged learning in the classroom. Involving students in learning as a dynamic process, a process that encourages critically reflective thinking and action oriented toward effecting socially just outcomes is multicultural education at its best (Bartolomé, 1994; Clark, 1997; Giroux, 1992b; Howard, 1993; Macedo, 1994; Mathison & Young, 1995; McCall, 1995; McIntosh, 1983; Nieto, 1996; Pinar, 1997).

More specific references to the need for multicultural education are seen in other of Arboleda's classroom experiences. In chapter 7, Arboleda mentions the test bias of standardized tests, specifically the Iowa Test of Basic Skills, and their negative impact on teachers' perception of him as a capable learner (or rather, as not a capable learner) as well as its correspondingly negative impact on his perception of himself as a learner. A growing body of research (Fair Test, see Part III; Nieto, 1996) continues to reinforce the conclusion that standardized tests at best measure a student's test-taking skills and at worst their adeptness in short-term rote memorization. This research concludes that these tests do virtually nothing to measure students' sustained retention of content area information nor their ability to think critically about, to analyze, to debate, to apply, to use such information in ways that are relevant to their past, current, and future personal, academic, and professional lives (Fair Test, see Part III; Nieto, 1996). If the stated, if not practiced, goal of education is to prepare students to become meaningful participants in a democratic society, standardized tests contribute absolutely nothing toward helping educators to help students reach that goal (Bartolomé, 1994; Clark, 1997; Giroux, 1992b; Howard, 1993; Macedo, 1994; Mathison & Young, 1995; McCall, 1995; McIntosh, 1983; Nieto, 1996; Pinar, 1997). Arboleda's critique of standardized tests, coupled with a review of the literature on alternative assessment strategies, may encourage all educators, but especially teacher educators and both their preservice and inservice teacher education students, to rethink the issue of testing and evaluation in significant detail, including their own methods of evaluation of student learning. A wonderful resource for such research and dialogue, just cited, is the Fair Test: National Center for Fair and Open Testing. In addition to providing clear, concise, and cogent critique of standardized testing based on broad-based, long-term, and high integrity studies, they provide legal assistance to educators interested in fighting district, state, and national standardized testing regulations. They also have resources that discuss standardized testing as big business, thereby revealing the political and economic nature of the beast that makes it both so difficult to slay and yet so worthy of attempting to do so.

In chapters 14 and 17, Arboleda also makes several references to the need for multicultural educational reform vis-à-vis content, pedagogy, and materials. With respect to content, he talks about the utter lack of information offered in the classroom that spoke to any of his life experiences, especially as Asian and even more so as a person from many cultures. Most of his K–12 curriculum content, even in Japan, focused on what peoples of European descent did and/or contributed to the world, society at large, as well as to specific academic subject areas. Mention of "Other" peoples was simply in terms of how they were appropriated by Europeans toward the Europeans' ends as indentured servants and slaves, or how they were simply extinguished by Europeans (or assassins thereof) for being "resistant" to "civilization" and hence "in the way," or "savage" and hence "too dangerous to allow to persist." This goes back to the notion of "reversals of truth" as discussed in chapter 3 and 4 of this guide (Daly, 1990; Welsing, 1970; see footnote 3 in chap. 3). In chapter 17, with respect to Arboleda's university level film and literature classes, he talks about the out-and-out racism on the part of both educators and classmates manifest in their unwillingness to include the perspectives of People of Color, women, Gays and Lesbians, and so forth, no matter how highly relevant their perspectives were to the course content.

With respect to pedagogy, Arboleda makes subtle references, in chapters 7 and 10, respectively, to the differences in how teachers he had in the United States and at least one that he had in Japan handled his name. In the United States, he returns home from school one day wanting to change both his skin color and name after bearing the repeated humiliation of having a teacher constantly mispronounce his name. In Japan, he sits in a classroom lamenting the point at which the teacher will inevitably mispronounce his name subsequently causing his classmates to laugh at him. To his surprise and relief, the teacher pronounces his name flawlessly. Although taking the time to learn how to pronounce a student's name correctly, with appropriate accent, and so forth, may seem insignificant, from the perspective of multicultural education, it may be the single most important thing any teacher can do (Nieto, 1996). Names are a key component of a person's identity, who they are, what family they come from. Names convey ethnicity, culture, heritage, language, religious affiliation, relationships, honor, and so much more. They are also often the teacher's first contact with a students and a student's first impression of a teacher. A teacher's attention to this detail can set a tone of respect or disrespect for how difference will be addressed in the classroom that can last an entire school year, positively or negatively effecting a student's school experience and academic success from that point forward (Nieto, 1996).

With respect to materials, in chapter 14, Arboleda talks repeatedly about especially young Japanese women struggling to learn English as a second language (ESL) with limited access to native speakers for practice. After resisting the demands placed on him to become a tutor-in-residence so to speak, Arboleda finally gives in. When he has the opportunity to review the ESL textbooks these young women are assigned in an effort to learn English, he realizes why they are so quick to abandon them in favor of conversation with people like himself. Arboleda articulates that the situational conversations depicted in the texts are largely irrelevant, they have no real life use or purpose in the English speaking world, that is, they are not realistic conversations that English speakers would have in any context. Furthermore, Arboleda points out, the topics of conversations the texts give as examples are out of date, not contemporary, wholly irrelevant to the students' life experiences. Engaging in dialogue with native English speakers on topics relevant to their "everyday" is far more productive in helping them to develop English fluency (García & Baker, 1995; Morales, 1996; Nieto, 1996).

Another tenet of multicultural education is that education must be meaningful to students. Because students constantly change, curriculum content, pedagogy, and materials must change in a symbiotic manner in order to be effective

(Bartolomé, 1994; Clark, 1997; Giroux, 1992b; Howard, 1993; Macedo, 1994; Mathison & Young, 1995; McCall, 1995; McIntosh, 1983; Nieto, 1996; Pinar, 1997). Although there is no recipe or prescription for how to develop multicultural education content, pedagogy, and materials, there are some parameters that can facilitate educators in developing multicultural curriculum (Clark, 1993a, 1993b).

The development of multicultural curriculum content must focus on revising Eurocentric curriculum content to include the representation of those traditionally under- or altogether unrepresented in it (People of Color, people of every ethnicity other than Anglo Saxon, second language speakers of English, working-class people, women, Lesbian and Gay people, physically, developmentally, and emotionally differently abled people, people of every religion other than Christian, especially Protestant, people under 21 and over 65 years of age, people who are not reasonably thin or attractive, people from everywhere but the East Coast of the United States, and environmentally concerned people, among others), as well as on innovating completely new curriculum that, from its inception, is already multiculturally inclusive (Clark, 1993a, 1993b). There are four parameters that may guide both the revision and innovation processes (Clark, 1993a, 1993b). The first parameter focuses on oppression, the second on lives, cultures, and countries of origin, the third on contributions and works, and the fourth on designers and implementers. With respect to all four of these parameters, it is important to note that changes made in curricula content must be comprehensive. To get students to understand a mathematical concept we do not give them one example and expect them to have grasped it; on the contrary we give them several examples. This is because just as with tokenism in employment, tokenism in the curriculum does not work. For students to truly grasp the concept of multiculturalism, as discussed in chapter 3 of this guide, they must be presented with a multiplicity of examples of it that are well integrated into all the curriculum to which they are exposed throughout their educational tenure.

Within the first parameter, the experiences of oppression of the traditionally underrepresented are emphasized, for example, as previously mentioned in chapter 4 of this guide, the enslavement of Africans by Europeans. But, although it is very important to detail histories of oppression, it is equally important to detail information about the lives, cultures, and countries of origin of those oppressed. This second parameter is particularly critical because to detail only a person's or a peoples' oppression leaves them at the level of victim or object, lacking authorship, agency, or subjectivity in their own lives. Understanding the everyday life, cultural traditions, and economic, social, political, and geographic conditions of existence, among other things, of a person or people is what affords them this authorship, agency, and subjectivity. But this understanding must not be superficial. That is, it must not illustrate another person or people as exotic, fantastic or peculiar; rather it must illustrate them as "regular people." Their day-to-day existence, practices, and environment must be presented as as normal to them as ours are to us, whoever the "they" and whoever the "we" are.

Within the third parameter, the contributions that underrepresented peoples have made to everyone's everyday lives, to all academic disciplines, and to the professional world, that we assign credit for to members of overrepresented groups, that we take for granted, and/or that we know nothing of, must be articulated. This includes their theories, inventions, equations and the like. And too, we must use and teach about their works; use their textbooks, novels, and poetry, and teach about their films, music, art, and so on. But, in accordance with the fourth parameter, it should not be only "us" or members of overrepresented peoples who teach about the underrepresented with respect to any or all of the first three parameters. Underrepresented peoples should likewise be designing and implementing curricula about themselves as well as about everything else.

In some ways, this last parameter supports Freire's (1970) contention that, "It would be a contradiction in terms if the oppressors not only defended but actually implemented a liberating education" (p. 39). This is because, "The oppressors, who oppress, exploit, and rape by virtue of their own power, cannot find in this power the strength to liberate either the oppressed or themselves" (p. 28). "Conditioned by the experience of oppressing others . . . any restriction on this way of life . . . appears to [them] as a profound violation of their individual rights . . . " (p. 43). " . . . the greatest humanistic and historical task of the oppressed" then, is "to liberate themselves and their oppressors . . . " as only their power "will be sufficiently strong to free both" (p. 28).

However, precisely because of the existence of the condition of overrepresentation, often there are only members of overrepresented groups present to design and implement such curricula (Clark, 1993a, 1993b). In addition, it should not be assumed that a member of an underrepresented group will necessarily design and implement such curricula for any number of reasons. Such reasons may range from their not possessing the knowledge to do so (just because they are a member of an underrepresented group does not automatically make them a multicultural curriculum development specialist), to their not wanting to call attention to themselves, to their not being supportive of such, and so on (Fanon, 1967; Freire, 1970; Laing & Cooper, 1971; Nieto, 1996; Sartre, 1976; Szasz, 1970). What is most important is that the designing and implementing of multicultural curricula is being done by someone genuinely supportive of and knowledgeable about multicultural education (Clark, 1993a, 1993b). In some circumstances it is necessary for this to be done only and always by a person from an underrepresented group. It can be inappropriate and largely impossible for a member of an overrepresented group to attempt to educate members of an underrepresented group about aspects of their history that, because of her or his experience as a member of an overrepresented group, she or he cannot fully understand (Freire, 1970). But, in other circumstances it is necessary for this to be done, at least initially, only by a member of an overrepresented group. It would be wholly unlikely to even find a single Person of Color in an exceptionally racist school district (Tatum, 1994). Ideally, however, this should be done by members of under and overrepresented groups together (Gussin Paley, 1979; Howard, 1993; Nieto, 1996).

In the final analysis, to be the most successful in revolutionizing curricula content in this and other manners, we especially need genuinely multiculturally supportive White male role models (Clark, 1993a, 1993b; Clark & O'Donnell,

1999a; McIntosh, 1992). Because of their power and conditioned by it, many will follow their lead in this endeavor who will not follow the same lead championed by any of the underrepresented (Pfeil, 1995). This is a function of the fact that White men are perceived to support any initiative for the "objective" good it will do all people, whereas the underrepresented are seen as supporting only those initiatives that will promote their own "agenda" (Marx, 1904).

Once educators have a sense of how to develop multicultural curricula content they will need to implement it. Having gone the distance to develop this state-of-the-art curricula content they cannot revert to Eurocentric strategies to implement it and expect to achieve its full effectiveness (Clark 1993a, 1993b).

Multicultural education pedagogy must focus on ways to provide students with a vast array of alternatives to the traditional didactic Eurocentric pedagogy to address differences in their learning styles (Bartolomé, 1994; Bigelow et. al, 1994; Clark, 1997; Gay, 1990; Giroux, 1992b; hooks, 1989, 1990; Howard, 1993; Macedo, 1994; Mathison & Young, 1995; McCall, 1995; McIntosh, 1983; Nieto, 1996; Pinar, 1997; Rosenberg, 1997; Thompson & Tyagi, 1993; Weinstein & Obear, 1992). There are ten parameters that may guide educators in providing this (Clark, 1993a, 1993b). The first four parameters focus on teaching philosophy, the organization of the learning environment, the assessment of student needs, and the use of organizational tools. The other six parameters focus on varying the instructional materials and their use, the instructional model, the instructional strategies, the learning activities, and the methods by which student learning and teaching effectiveness are assessed.

First and in accordance with Freire's (1970) research, teachers must give up the notion of teaching as mastery. Although teacher education often "trains" rather than educates one to think of oneself as a master of one's discipline, this training is in large measure Eurocentric. Given this, at best a teacher could only be a monocultural master of their discipline, highly skilled at imparting knowledge about their academic specialty from a largely Eurocentric perspective. Even a teacher who is highly multiculturally competent in their subject area or discipline could not really be considered a multicultural master of it because so much of the multicultural information in every discipline has been obscured historically that what we have only begun to uncover today is likely but a fraction of what there is to know. As our classrooms become increasingly diverse, we must confront the reality that our students will undoubtedly have more knowledge about particular subjects and disciplines than we do simply because of their different life experiences, although, at the same time, we should not assume that they do just because of these life experiences.

Given all this, it makes more sense to think of ourselves as facilitators of the process of learning and actively involve students in this process. To do this we must begin by asking students what they already know about a particular subject to make sure that the information they are exposed to is new and at a level that challenges them, as well as to demonstrate to them that they already have knowledge about many things of which they may be unaware. We must also ask them what they want to learn about a subject (Freire, 1970).

With this mindset and information in hand, we can engage students in a dialogue by posing questions to them that cause them to think critically, relative to knowledge that they already possess, in order to arrive at answers to questions about new bodies of information. In this way we no longer look on students and they no longer see themselves as empty receptacles into which we make deposits of information, but rather as critical agents in their own education (Freire, 1970).

Second, teachers must be attentive to the impact of the physical and aesthetic organization of the immediate educational environment on learning. For example, is the classroom clean and neat? Should the chairs be set up in a circle or desks in work stations rather than rows to best facilitate learning? Do the pictures on the wall and the resources in the classroom affirm the experiences of all the students in it as well as those they may meet in the world beyond?

Third, teachers must vary the methods by which they assess student needs. For example, they can alternate the use of written assessment tests, computerized assessment tests, student oral or written self-assessment with peers, teachers, or parents, or teacher observation (Fair Test, see Part III).

Fourth, teachers must use organizational tools. For example, they can use a "weekly format" that is consistent: every Monday review reading assignments, every Wednesday have a class discussion, and so on. They can use a "daily format," by beginning each class collecting homework, then introducing new information, and so on. They can use "motivators" to get the immediate attention of students at the beginning of a class, such as wearing a top hat to class the day they discuss the fashion of a particular historical period. Similarly, they can use "closers" to signal the end of class, like a review of important discussion points. In addition to the syllabus, they can provide students with an agenda for each class so that students will know what is going to happen that day. They can also use handouts to help students structure their notes from assigned readings or that define key concepts or technical vocabulary in those readings with which students may be unfamiliar.

Fifth, teachers must use an array of instructional materials. These can include texts, books, newspapers, journals, audiotapes, workbooks, games, magazines, plays, videotapes, Internet resources, and so forth. However, before such materials are employed, teachers must assess them for potential bias. The Council on Interracial Books for Children has published several guides (see Part III) to assist teachers in evaluating their instructional materials for racial, ethnic, linguistic, gender, and other biases and/or discrimination. The "Teaching Tolerance" arm of the Southern Poverty Law Center also has published resources (see Part III), many of them free, to assist teachers in this respect. The materials selected should be as bias-free as possible, and varied enough to, when taken collectively, positively affirm the experiences of each and every student in the classroom, at the same time, when considered individually, disaffirm none.

Sixth, teachers must vary the use of instructional materials. For example, they can use texts that have multiculturally representative pictures, names, situations and language; they can use Eurocentric texts and encourage students to think critically about, dissect, question what is being presented; they can not use texts at all and use a variety of other resources instead; or they can use all of these materials in combination.

Seventh, teachers must vary the instructional model. For example, they can use a thematic approach in which students are encouraged to look for recurrent trends in U.S. history. Or they can use an interdisciplinary approach to teach philosophy in which students are encouraged to understand how the economic situation, political climate, geographic location, and cultural traditions of a people or an era influenced the development of a particular branch of philosophic discourse.

Eighth, teachers must vary their instructional strategies. For example, they can have students engage in whole class discussions, small group work, partner work, individual work, one-on-one work with the teacher, peer teaching and learning, student teaching of the whole class, or debate.

Ninth, teachers must vary the learning activities. For example, they can have students engage in assignments that require them to develop and employ in varied measure affective, cognitive, and motor skills through reading, writing, speaking, listening, or problem solving initiatives.

Tenth, teachers must vary the methods by which they evaluate student learning and, hence, teaching effectiveness. For example, they can vary the use essay tests, oral tests, term papers, or creative projects.

Another part of this last parameter, students should be engaged in self-evaluation of their academic effort and performance. When involved in this way, students are amazingly honest about what they think their grade should be and are less inclined to express animosity to a teacher for giving them a grade they do not like precisely because they had a hand in determining it and therefore know what it is before it comes in the mail (Fair Test, see Part III; Freire, 1970).

Students should also be involved in the evaluation of the course content, the instructional materials, and the teaching of it, as well as in making recommendations for improving it the next time it is taught. In this way they become more invested in learning because they have helped to determine what and how they learned while simultaneously becoming better at learning as they become more aware of their learning style and of how to prepare differently for evaluation in different subject areas and by different methods. This also has the effect of improving the quality of instruction because student feedback lets the teacher know directly what did and did not work. In so doing it encourages teachers to continually revise and refine the teaching of a subject they teach, making it and them ever-fresh in the process and perpetuating the dialectical and reciprocal nature of teaching and learning (Freire, 1970).

In general, learning must be made more active, interactive, and experiential. This is confirmed by Kunjufu's (1995) research in which he found that most male students regardless of race, but especially most Black male students, learn best when learning activities are shifted every 20 minutes. So, for example, the first 20 minutes of a class might be a short film, followed by 20 minutes of discussion, and then perhaps a 20 minute writing assignment summarizing the film and pertinent discussion points.

Certainly, Kunjufu (1995) points out, although this organization may most favor the learning style of most Black male students, all students will benefit from exposure to it in some ways. This is particularly true for all female students, especially White ones, who have been socialized to be passive learners (American Association of University Women, see Part III; Nieto, 1996;

Wellesley Center for Research on Women, see Part III). There are two fundamental reasons why multicultural education focuses, in particular, on varying methods of implementing curricula content rather than trying to teach a particular way to particular groups of students. The first is because not all students in a particular group learn *the* way their group is said to learn (i.e., stereotypically versus characteristically as discussed in chapter 2 of this guide). The second is because all students benefit from exposure to multifaceted approaches as such challenges them to broaden their repertoire for learning in some ways while affirming their preferred learning style in others (Nieto, 1996).

Researchers at the University of California at Berkeley (Asera, 1988) also pointed to the importance of creating a learning interest "culture" to facilitate students in broadening their repertoire for learning at the same time effecting positive cross-cultural interaction between students. In a series of studies these researchers found that White students normally associate with other White students who are performing at the same academic level regardless of learning interest. Here peer associations were founded on similarities in race and academic performance. A low-achieving White student in biology would tend to associate with a low-achieving White student in English, whereas a high-achieving White student in physics would tend to recreate with a high-achieving White student in history. On the other hand, they found that Students of Color normally associate with other Students of Color (and most often those from their own racial, and within this their own ethnic, group) regardless of academic level or learning interest. Here, peer associations were founded essentially on similarities in race only. A low achieving Black student in philosophy would tend to associate with a moderate achieving Black student in chemistry and a high achieving Black student in art.

In creating a learning interest "culture," through the development and implementation of "workshops" where an individual student's evaluation is based on the collective performance of their workshop group members, students come to associate with other students with the same learning interests as themselves regardless of race or academic performance. This has had the overall effect of enhancing the academic performance of all the students across the learning interest, encouraging the development of cross-cultural relationships and peer teaching, and ultimately broadening the repertoire for learning of all involved (Asera, 1988). Not surprisingly, this initiative has also had the effect of reducing racial tensions on the school, college, and university campuses where it is employed (Asera, 1988; McLean-Donaldson, 1996).

It is important to note that Kunjufu (1995), although supportive of multicultural education, is more supportive of African American malecentric education and afrocentric or Africancentric education, not for all students like Eurocentric education has been applied, but for Black male students and all Black students, respectively. And here Kunjufu is not alone as Latina and Latino centric, specifically Puerto Rican, educational models and schools have been championed as well. These initiatives, some of which are branches of and others precursors to multicultural education, have developed in direct response to not only schools' resistance to dealing with issues of diversity, but especially to developing and implementing multicultural curricula (Bollin & Finkel, 1995;

Dyson, 1993; Fanon, 1963; Franklin, 1966; Gray, 1995; Hacker, 1992; hooks, 1992; Hutchinson, 1994; Kovel; 1984; Loiacano, 1989; Morrison, 1992; McCarthy & Critchlow, 1993; McIntosh, 1989).

Although it may be wonderful to talk about the pluralistic process of developing and implementing multicultural education curriculum content, pedagogy, and materials, and of building multicultural schools, as well as to participate in both, the stark reality, to which Arboleda's experience points, is that these schools are needed not only now, but yesterday, last year, a decade ago, a century ago. This is because there have already been too many casualties, students lost because they were "educated" by the "methods employed by the oppressor [which] deny pedagogical action in the liberation process" (Freire, 1970, p. 55). There are more of these casualties happening as we speak and still more waiting to happen at some future moment (Bollin & Finkel, 1995; Dyson, 1993; Fanon, 1963; Franklin, 1966; Gray, 1995; Hacker, 1992; hooks, 1992; Hutchinson, 1994; Kovel; 1984; Loiacano, 1989; McCarthy & Critchlow, 1993; McIntosh, 1989; Morrison, 1992). And yet, we must still champion multicultural education over all forms of centrism because, reminiscent of the Booker T. Washington/W.E.B DuBois debate, we know that separate, whether by imposition or choice, never means equal (Kunjufu, 1995).

Perhaps Arboleda's pondering as a child as to whether or not frogs in Parkway could communicate with frogs in Tokyo is as powerful an example of the need for multicultural education as any. The sentiment in his pondering here is echoed in another child's question to a teacher in a bilingual classroom as to whether or not God is bilingual (obviously and so unfortunately not a classroom located anywhere in the state of California given the recent antibilingual education edict passed there; Ang, 1995; García & Baker, 1995; Morales, 1996). Certainly, if people pray in all languages God must not only be bilingual but multilingual the teacher responded; and hence decidedly supportive of multicultural education one might add. Ultimately, the goal of multicultural education is "to make the 'other' 'us' and not 'them'" (Rorty, 1989). This is the essence of Arboleda's struggle, to become a part of "us" (ironically also, the United States), an affirmingly multicultural "us," eradicating "them" and "Otherness" altogether.

NOTES

[1]Black students were, in fact, treated poorly when they were the few among the many Whites in predominantly White schools; conversely, and despite *perceptions* to the contrary, Whites were generally treated very well when they were the few among the many Blacks in the predominantly Black schools. The latter had to be the case because if anything negative were to happen to a White person in a predominantly Black school or the surrounding community, it would be at the expense of not only the individual White person but the entire Black community— the members of which would be collectively held responsible and subsequently subject to intense retaliation manifest in the form of brutal police harassment (Public Broadcasting System, 1992).

6

Suggestions for How to Use
In the Shadow of Race
in the Multicultural Education,
Race-Related Education,
and General Studies Classroom

Arboleda's *In the Shadow of Race*, may be adapted for a wide array of courses. Clearly, is it highly relevant for multicultural education courses in teacher education programs. It is also highly relevant for first-year student orientation courses, common on many college and university campuses, which serve to introduce students to the concept of cultural diversity. Many of these orientation courses are a part of a single "diversity requirement," whereas others may count as one of several required "viewing the wider world" courses (Bensimon & Soto, 1997; Elfin, 1993; Gallagher, 1994; Hardiman & Jackson, 1992; Tatum, 1992).

In the multicultural education course, *In the Shadow of Race* is appropriate as a supplemental text. In particular, it would compliment Sonia Nieto's, *Affirming Diversity: The Sociopolitical Context of Multicultural Education* (1996), Karen McLean-Donaldson's already mentioned, *Through Students Eyes: Racism in United States' Schools* (1996), and Bill Bigelow et. al., *Rethinking Our Classrooms: Teaching for Equity and Justice* (1994), among others (see Part III). In the student orientation course, *In the Shadow of Race* could stand alone as the single text for such. It is an excellent introductory text for students never before formally exposed to issues of cultural diversity.

But, *In the Shadow of Race* is also an excellent supplementary resource for race-related courses like race relations, the psychology of racism, and cross-cultural relations, counseling, and/or social work as well as more general social studies/history, government/political science, sociology, and even geography courses. In fact, for educators just beginning to integrate a multicultural perspective into courses such as these, *In the Shadow of Race* is an excellent first resource in this regard both in terms of the content it provides as well as from a pedagogical perspective in using the autobiography as a starting point for all learning (hooks, 1993).

In race-related courses, *In the Shadow of Race* can be used to look at the global nature of racism, especially issues of culturally-related conflict and violence both in the United States and abroad with respect to race, ethnicity, nationality, citizenship, heritage, and religion. Such courses could be structured around the events Arboleda discusses. For example, the Civil Rights Movement (chap. 7) as previously discussed in Part II chapter 5.

Psychology of racism courses could focus students on Arboleda's family's and friends' psychological struggle with racism and other forms of discrimination. In particular, the rage of his paternal grandmother and grandfather, his mother and father, his brother, his friend Ukumbra, and of his own and all of their longing to belong, as previously discussed in chapter 1 of this guide. The internalized self-hatred racism brought to bear on these same individuals, as well as on whole cultures as Arboleda describes in relationship to the Japanese. Also, the more severe episodes of psychological disassociation of his paternal grandmother while in the Phillipines as well as of his own while homeless. The Southern Poverty Law Center's, *History of Hate in the United States* video (1995) would be an excellent supplementary resource here. It would also help to locate this kind of discussion in a sociopolitical and sociohistorical context, thereby mitigating the pathologizing effect of a Eurocentrically conceptualized psychoanalyses of Arboleda, his family, and his friends as targets of racism and discrimination, by correctly reassigning the characterization of pathological to the perpetrators, the Europeans (Jackson & Hardiman, 1988; Laing & Cooper, 1971; Sue, 1990; Szasz, 1970).

Cross-cultural relations, counseling, and/or social work courses could take advantage of all of the cross-cultural comparisons that Arboleda either makes himself or provides the reader to draw for her or himself from the information and detail his narrative provides. For example, cross-cultural differences in terms of how time, respect, honor, friendship, commitment, family, conversation norms, etiquette, work ethic, among many things are conceptualized (chaps. 14 through 18). Analysis of conflicts that emerge in many relationships Arboleda details in terms of cross-cultural misunderstanding would make for rich discussion. These relationships could even be delineated on genograms or ecomaps (Lipsitz, 1996; Sue, 1990; Thomas & Sillen, 1972).

In social studies/history courses, *In the Shadow of Race* could be used by tracing Arboleda's ancestry chronologically (as he tells it) or thematically. The chronological could involve tracking each ancestor (grandma, grandpa, oma, opa, mother, father, brother's spouse, brother, author's spouse, and author), from birth to death or present day. World War II and the Vietnam war could be used as thematic points of reference as discussed in chapter 1 of this guide. The colonization of Korea, China, and Hokkaido by the Japanese (chap. 13), of the Phillipines by the Spanish (chap. 2), of North America by the English, Spanish, French, Germans, Dutch, and so forth (chaps. 14 and 17) could also be used as thematic points of reference. Excellent supplementary resources for these discussion may be found in Loewen (1995), Takaki (1993), and Zinn (1980) as previously cited in Part II chapter 5, as well as Facing History and Ourselves (see Part III).

In government/political science courses, *In the Shadow of Race* might support discussions of fascism (Germany, chaps. 3 through 5), capitalism (the United States and Japan, chaps. 17 through 23), and communism (Eastern Europe, chaps. 3, 6, & 24), as well as political policy development (manifest destiny, *Brown versus the Board of Education of Topeka* as discussed in Part II chap. 5 of this guide, and U.S./Phillipines relations, and their impact on Filipina and Filipino immigration to the United States as alluded to in chap. 1 of this guide). A number of books published by Monthly Review Press would particularly support these types of discussions (see Part III).

In sociology courses, certainly *In the Shadow of Race* could help highlight discussions on an array of social problems in the United States and abroad. The contradictions between Arboleda's often privileged class status juxtaposed with his tormented race and ethnic location virtually everywhere that he and his family live would make for one interesting area of analysis in this regard (chaps. 6 through 8, & 21). Arboleda also makes numerous references to the marketing of blonde haired, blue eyed, thin but well-endowed White women the world over vis-à-vis the hit television series *Baywatch*, posters, fashion and smut magazines, and department store mannequins (chaps. 10, 11, & 15) as discussed previously in this guide. This might make for another interesting area of analysis, especially one specifically related to global racism and sexism proliferated by the U.S. media and big business. The video "Dreamworlds II" (Jhally, 1996; Media Educational Foundation, 1996) is an excellent supplementary resource for this latter analysis.

Finally, in geography courses, *In the Shadow of Race* could be adopted to facilitate the learning of global geography in the context of sociopolitical changes. For example, Arboleda's trip to Eastern Europe (detailed in chap. 24) could lead to a discussion of national boundary issues. His discussion of the Phillipines (in chap. 2) opens up the opportunity for dialogue on industrialization in different geographic areas of the world. Arboleda also discusses the concept of westernization with respect to the Phillipines (chap. 2), Hokkaido (chap. 13), and Japan (chaps. 10 through 15), and immigration issues with respect to Germany (chaps. 3 through 6, 10, & 24), the United States (chaps. 18, 19, & 21), and Japan (chaps. 12 & 14), both of which also lend themselves to a geographic point of entry into debate. Again, a number of the books published by Monthly Review Press would particularly support these types of discussions (see Part III).

Obviously, the possibilities for stimulating dialogue and debate with *In the Shadow of Race* in virtually any course on virtually any topic are practically endless. Furthermore, problem-posing questions can be formulated for many of the situations related in the text in manners also highly relevant to each of the subject areas aforereferenced.

For example, in a race relations course, the question could be posed as to why all of the students in Arboleda's school in Japan sat in race-segregated groups in the lunchroom but moved more freely between and among different racial groups when interacting in other contexts (chap. 10). The supplemental text, *Why are all the Black Kids Sitting Together in the Cafeteria?* and *Other Conversations about Race*, by Beverly Daniel Tatum (1997) could be used to support and further develop this conversation.

In a psychology of racism course, the question of how racism negatively impacts the mental health of each member of Arboleda's family could be explored (chaps. 2, 7, 14, & 19). This question could then be turned on its head and redirected at Whites by asking how perpetrating racism negatively impacts them. The texts, *Counseling the Culturally Different: Theory and Practice* (Sue, 1990) and *Impacts of Racism on White Americans* (Bowser & Hunt, 1981) could be used to tease out difficult issues for discussion related to both of these questions.

In cross-cultural relations, counseling, and/or social work courses, students could debate answers to the question as to how they imagine Arboleda, his brother, his mother, his father, and his father's second wife cope with the second wife's cultural tradition requiring Arboleda's father to cut all contact with his first wife and any children he had with her (chaps. 19 & 20). The follow-up questions: What, if any, compromises might be suggested given cross-cultural norms and expectations? How might you as a counselor or social worker address this conflict if this family became your client?

In a social studies/history course students might be asked to consider: What are the sociopolitical ramifications of Arboleda's paternal grandfather's "change" in "race" or rather racial reassignment from Asian to White? (chap. 2). To supplement this discussion, students might explore Ian Haney López's, *White By Law: The Legal Construction of Race* (1996) and Noel Ignatiev's, *How the Irish Became White* (1995; see also the discussion on race as a construction in chap. 3 of this guide), and compare and contrast the experiences of other individuals and whole peoples whose racial and ethnic identities hinged and continue to hinge on biological, social, legal, and otherwise political constructions of these social membership group categorizations.

Government/political science students could consider questions regarding racial categorization. For example: What, if any, impact could be expected if the U.S. census suddenly no longer recorded citizen's race and all existing records of such were abolished? (chaps. 21, 22, & 24). What, if any, impact might this have on Affirmative Action and Equal Employment and Equal Education Opportunity legislation? (see also the discussion related to this latter issue in chap. 2 of this guide; Edsall & Edsall, 1992; Flagg, 1993; Jenkins, 1994).

Students of Sociology might struggle with the questions: What is the ultimate cost to a society of any form of supremacy? What has been and continues to be the cost of White supremacy in the United States both domestically and internationally? What is the cost of White supremacy in the United States to both People of Color and Whites? In what ways are these costs the same for both People of Color and Whites and in what ways are they different? (Fishkin, 1995; Gould, 1996; Haney López, 1996; Kovel, 1984; Kozol, 1991; Nieto, 1998; Novick, 1995; Oakes, 1985; Powell, 1996; Terkel, 1992; Terry, 1981; Thompson, 1996; Welsing, 1970; see also the discussion on racial power dynamics in chap. 3 in this guide). What are the costs of White supremacy in the United States, manifest through the hidden Eurocentric curriculum, to all students? (Banks, 1991, 1992, 1994a, 1994b; Bigelow, 1990; Clark, 1993a; hooks, 1993; Nieto, 1996, 1998; Oakes, 1985; Schwartz, 1993; Shor, 1992; Sleeter & Grant, 1991; Sleeter, 1996; Walsh, 1991; see also the discussion on Eurocentrism in education in Part II chap. 5 of this guide).

Lastly, in geography courses students might consider the question: What is the impact of a geographic border (the "Other" side of the tracks, the "Other" side of an international border, and so forth) on a person or a people's quality of life? An excellent advanced supplementary resource for this discussion is Henry Giroux's, *Border Crossings: Cultural Workers and the Politics of Education* (1992a; see also the discussion on racial borderlands in chap. 3 of this guide).

Perhaps the most provocative question *In the Shadow of Race* begs is a question adaptable to any course: How does one develop the awareness, knowledge, understanding, motivation, and commitment to become successful in interacting with dignity and respect across multiple cultures so as not to lose one's own identity at the same time not compromising the identities of others? Paulo Freire (1970) described this process as that of "becoming more fully human." It is toward that end that *In the Shadow of Race* and this supplementary guide are dedicated to facilitating.

PART III
Bibliography

7

References and Additional Resources[1]

Adams, M., Bell, L. A., & Griffin, P. (Eds.). (1997). *Teaching for diversity and social justice: A sourcebook.* New York: Routledge.

Alba, R. D. (1990). *Ethnic identity: The transformation of White America* New Haven: Yale University Press.

*Allen, T. (1994). *The invention of the White race.* London: Verso.

Allen, W. B. (1993). Response to "White discourse on White racism." *Educational Researcher, 22*(8), 11–13.

Allport, G. W. (1958). *The nature of prejudice.* Reading, MA: Addison-Wesley.

Alpert, H. (1995). *The lonely bull* (Remake). New York: MCA Records/BMG Entertainment.

American Association of University Women, 1111 16th Street, N. W., Washington, D. C. 20036. P(800) 821-4364, F(202) 872-1425. www.aauw.org.

Ang, I. (1995). On not speaking chinese: Postmodern ethnicity and the politics of diaspora. *Social Formations, 24,* 110–121.

Angus, I. (1990, Spring-Summer). Crossing the border. *Massachusetts Review, 32–47.*

Anzaldua, G. (1987). *Borderlands/la frontera: The new Mestiza.* San Francisco: Spinsters/Aunt Lute.

Apple, M. W. (1997). Consuming the Other: Whiteness, education, and cheap french fries. In M. Fine, L. Weis, L. C. Powell, & L. M. Wong (Eds.), *Off white: Readings on race, power, and society,* pp. 121–128. New York: Routledge.

Arboleda, T. (1990). Ethnic man! [video]. Boston: Entertaining Diversity.

Arboleda, T. (1998). *In the shadow of race: Growing up as a multiethnic, multicultural, and "multiracial" American.* Mahwah, NJ: Lawrence Erlbaum Associates.

Asera, R. (1988). *The workshop model.* Unpublished manuscript. University of California, Berkeley, Professional Development Program.

Association of Black Psychologists, P. O. Box 55999, Washington, D. C. 20040.

Balibar, E. (1996). Is European citizenship possible? *Public Culture, 19,* 355–376.

Banks, J. A. (1991). *Teaching strategies for ethnic studies.* Boston: Allyn & Bacon.

Banks, J. A. (1992). The stages of ethnicity. In P. A. Richard-Amato & M. A. Snow (Eds.), *The multicultural classroom: Readings for the content-area teachers,* pp. 93–101. White Plains, NY: Longman.

Banks, J. A. (1994a). *An introduction to multicultural education.* Boston: Allyn & Bacon.

Banks, J. A. (1994b). *Multiethnic education: Theory and practice* (3rd Ed.). Needham Heights, MA: Allyn & Bacon.

Bartolomé, L. (1994). Beyond the methods fetish: Toward a humanizing pedagogy. *Harvard Educational Review, 64*(2), 173–194.

Batts, V. A. (1989). *Modern racism: New melody for the same old tunes.* Cambridge, MA: Visions.

Bell, B., Gaventa, J., & Peters, J. (Eds.). (1990). *We make the road by walking: Conversations on education and social change.* Philadelphia: Temple University Press.

Bell, D. (1992). *Faces at the bottom of the well: The permanence of racism.* New York: Basic Books.

Bell, D. (1995). Racial Realism—After we're gone: Prudent speculations on America in a post-racial epoch. In R. Delgado (Ed.), *Critical race theory: The cutting edge,* pp. 25–32. Philadelphia: Temple University Press.

Bengis, S. (1987). *Can the Navajo nation reclaim the swastika as a symbol of peace?: A psychological perspective.* Unpublished manuscript. The New England Adolescent Research Institute, Holyoke, Massachusetts.

Bensimon, E. M., & Soto, M. (1997). Can we build civic life without a multiracial university? *Change, 29*, 42–44.

Bennett, M. J. (1986). A developmental approach to training for intercultural sensitivity. *International Journal of Intercultural Relations, 10*, 179–196.

Berman, P. (Ed.). (1992). *Debating p.c.: The controversy over political correctness on college campuses*. New York: Dell.

Bhachu, P. (1996). The multiple landscapes of transnational Asian women in the diaspora. In V. Amit-Talai & C. Knowles (Eds.), *Re-Situating identities: The politics of race, ethnicity, and culture*, pp. 283–303. Peterborough, Canada: Broadview.

Bigelow, W. (1990). Inside the classroom: Social vision and critical pedagogy. *Teachers College Record, 91*(3), 437–448.

Bigelow, W., Christensen, L., Karp, S., Miner, B., & Petersen, B. (1994). *Rethinking our classrooms: Teaching for equity and justice*. Milwaukee, WI: Rethinking Schools.

100 Black Men of America, Inc., 141 Auburn Avenue, Atlanta, GA 30303. P(404) 688-5100.

Bollin, G. G., & Finkel, J. (1995). White racial identity as a barrier to understanding diversity: A study of preservice teachers. *Equity and Excellence in Education, 28*(1), 25–30.

Bonnett, A. (1996). Anti-racism and the critique of White identities. *New Community, 22*(1), 97–110.

Bourdieu, P., Passeron, J.-C., DeSaint Martin, M., Teese, R. (1996). *Academic discourse: Linguistic misunderstanding and professorial power*. Stanford, CA: Stanford University Press.

Bowen, A. (1993). *Political correctness and multiculturalism*. Unpublished manuscript. Clark University, Worcester, Massachusetts.

Bowles, S., & Gintis, H. (1977). *Schooling in capitalist America: Educational reform and the contradictions of economic life*. New York: Basic Books.

Bowser, B. P., & Hunt, R. G. (Eds.). (1981). *Impacts of racism on White Americans*. Beverly Hills: Sage.

Brenkman, J. (1995). Race publics: Civic illiberalism, or race after Reagan. *Transition, 5*(2), 14–27.

Brown, D. (1971). *Bury my heart at Wounded Knee: An Indian history of the American west.* New York: Holt & Rinehart.

Bulkin, E. (1984). Hard ground: Jewish identity, racism and anti-Semitism. In E. Bulkin, M. B. Pratt & B. Smith (Eds.), *Yours in struggle*, pp.73–82. Brooklyn: Long Haul.

Cashmore, E. (1996). *Dictionary of race and ethnic relations* (4th Ed.). New York: Routledge.

*Chan, C. S. (1989). Issues of identity development among Asian-American Lesbians and Gay men. *Journal of Counseling and Development, 68*(5), 16–20.

Chasnoff, D., & Cohen, H. (1996). It's elementary: Talking about Gay issues in schools [video]. Los Angeles: Women's Educational Media.

Clark, C. (1993a). *Multicultural education as a tool for disarming violence: A study through in-depth participatory action research.* Unpublished doctoral dissertation. University of Massachusetts, Amherst.

Clark, C. (1993b). Multicultural understanding across the curriculum, *Recruitment and Retention, 2*(7), 2–3.

Clark, C. (1997). The social construction of borders and trends towards their deconstruction: Implications for the pedagogical engagement of students identified as behaviorally special needs. *The Border Walking Journal, 1*(1), 1–10.

Clark, C. (1999). The secret: White lies are never little. In C. Clark & J. O'Donnell (Eds.), *Becoming and unbecoming White: Owning and disowning a racial identity*, pp. 92–113. Westport, CT: Greenwood.

Clark, C., & Jenkins, M. (1994). Multiculturalism as a policy for disarming gang violence in communities at large and schools, *ERIC Clearinghouse for Urban Education* (Doc. No. ED 368 813).

Clark, C., & O'Donnell, J. (Eds.). (1999a). *Becoming and unbecoming White: Owning and disowning a racial identity.* Westport, CT: Greenwood.

Clark, C., & O'Donnell, J. (1999b). Rearticulating a racial identity: Creating oppositional spaces to fight for equality and social justice. In C. Clark & J. O'Donnell (Eds.), *Becoming and unbecoming White: Owning and disowning a racial identity*, pp. 1–10. Westport, CT: Greenwood.

Clark, C., Jenkins, M., & Stowers, G. (in press). *Fear of da' gangsta': The social construction, production, and reproduction of violence in schools for corporate profit and the revolutionary promise of critical multicultural education.* Westport, CT: Greenwood.

Connolly, M. L. & Noumair, D. A. (1997). The White girl in me, the colored girl in you, and the Lesbian in us: Crossing boundaries. In M. Fine, L. Weis, L. C. Powell, & L. M. Wong (Eds.), *Off white: Readings on race, power, and society*, pp. 322–332. New York: Routledge.

Council on Interracial Books for Children, 1841 Broadway, New York, NY 10023.

Cross, Jr., W. E. (1973). The Negro-to-Black conversion experience. In J. A. Ladner (Ed.), *The death of White sociology*, pp. 267–286. New York: Vintage Books.

Cross, Jr., W. E. (1978). The Thomas and Cross models of psychological nigrescence: A review. *The Journal of Black Psychology*, 5(1), 13–31.

Cruz, J. (1996). From farce to tragedy: Reflections on the reification of race at century's end. In A. Gordon & C. Newfield (Eds.), *Mapping multiculturalism*, pp. 19–39. Minneapolis: University of Minnesota Press.

Daly, M. (1990). *Gyn/Ecology, the metethics of radical feminism: With a new intergalactic introduction*. Boston: Beacon Press.

Davis, A. Y. (1981). *Women, race and class*. New York: Random House.

Dean J. P., & Suchman, E. A. (1964). *Strangers next door: Ethnic relations in American communities*. Englewood Cliffs, NJ: Prentice-Hall.

Delgado, R. (Ed.). (1995). *Critical race theory: The cutting edge*. Philadelphia: Temple University Press.

Delgado, R., & Stefancic, J. (Eds.). (1997). *Critical White studies: Looking behind the mirror*. Philadelphia: Temple University Press.

Delinquent Habits (1995). *Trés delinquentes*. New York: MCA Records/BMG Entertainment.

Dennis, R. (1981). Socialization and racism: The White experience. In B. P. Bowser & R. G. Hunt (Eds.), *Impacts of racism on White Americans*, pp. 127–143. Beverly Hills: Sage.

Derman-Sparks, L., & A. B. C. Task Force. (1989). *Anti-bias curriculum: Tools for empowering young children*. Washington, DC: National Association for Young Children.

Donato, R. (1997). *The other struggle for equal schools: Mexican Americans during the civil rights era*. Albany: State University of New York Press.

Dott, Jr., R. H., & Batten, R. L. (1981). *Evolution of the earth*. New York: McGraw-Hill.

Douglas, F. (1972). The meaning of the fourth of July to the Negro. In P. S. Foner (Ed.), *The Voice of Black America (Vol. 1)*, pp. 127–146. New York: Capricorn Books.

*D'Souza, D. (1995). *The end of racism: Principles for a multiracial society*. New York: The Free Press.

DuBois, E. C., & Ruíz, V. L. (1990). *Unequal sisters: A multicultural reader in U.S. women's history*. New York: Routledge.

Dussell, E. (1993). Eurocentrism and modernity. *Boundary 2, 20*(3), 65–77.

Dyer, R. (1992). White. *Screen, 29*(4), 44–64.

Dyson, M. E. (1993). *Reflecting Black*. Minneapolis: University of Minnesota Press.

Edsall, T. B & Edsall, M. D. (1992). *Chain reactions: The impact of race, rights, and taxes on American politics*. New York: W. W. Norton.

The Education vs. Incarceration Clearinghouse (1998). [On-line]. Available: http://www.cjcj.org/clearinghouse.html.

Eflin, M. (1993, April 19). Race on campus. *U. S. News and World Report*, 52–56.

Ehrlich, H. J. (1994, June). Reporting ethnoviolence: Newspaper treatment of race and ethnic conflict. *Z Magazine*, 53–60.

Fair Test: National Center for Fair & Open Testing, 342 Broadway, Cambridge, MA 02139. P(617) 864-4810, F(617) 497-2224.

Fanon, F. (1963). *The wretched of the earth*. New York: Grove.

Fanon, F. (1967). *Black skin, White masks*. New York: Grove.

Facing History and Ourselves, Research and Resources for Educators and Friends, 16 Hurd Road, Brookline, MA 02146. P(617) 232-1595.

Feagin, J. R., & Vera, H. (1995). *White racism: The basics*. London: Routledge.

Flagg, B. (1993). "Was blind, but now I see": White race consciousness and the requirement of disciminatory intent, *Michigan Law Review, 91*(3), 953–1017.

Fishkin, S. F. (1995). Interrogating "whiteness," Complicating "blackness": Remapping American culture, *American Quarterly, 47*(3), 428–466.

Flores, J. (1993). *Divided borders: Essays on Puerto Rican identity.* Houston: Arte Publico.

Fordham, S. (1988). Racelessness as a factor in Black students' school success: Pragmatic strategy or pyrrhic victory? *Harvard Educational Review, 58*(1), 27–42.

Frankenberg, R. (1993a). *White women, Race matters.* Minneapolis: University of Minnesota Press.

Frankenberg, R. (1993b). *The social construction of whiteness.* Minneapolis: University of Minnesota Press.

Franklin, V. P. (1966). *Black self-determination, a cultural history of the faith of the fathers.* Westport, CT: Lawrence Hill & Company.

Freire, P. (1970). *Pedagogy of the oppressed.* New York: Seabury.

Friedman, S. S. (1995). Beyond White and Other: Relationality and narratives of race in feminist discourse. *Signs, 21*(1), 25–37.

Gallagher, C. A. (1994). White construction in the university. *Socialist Review, 1 & 2,* 165–187.

García, O. & Baker, C. (Eds.). (1995). *Policy and practice in bilingual education: Extending the foundations.* Avon, England: Multilingual Matters.

Gates, Jr., H. L. (Ed.) (1996). *Loose canons: Notes on the culture wars.* New York: Oxford University Press.

Gay, G. (1985). Implications of selected models of ethnic identity development for educators. *Journal of Negro Education, 54*(1), 43–55.

Gay, G. (1990). Achieving educational equality through curriculum desegregation. *Phi Delta Kappan, 4*(2), 56–62.

Geertz, C. (1973). *The interpretation of cultures.* New York: Basic Books.

*George, L. (1993, January 17). Gray boys, funky Aztecs and honorary homegirls. *The Los Angeles Times Magazine,* 14–19.

Gillan, M. (1992). Prejudice: Answering children's questions [video]. ABC News Special with Peter Jennings and ABC Science Editor, Micheal Gillan. New York: NYNEX Kids Now.

Giroux, H. A. (1977). *Channel surfing: Race talk and the destruction of today's youth.* New York: St. Martin's.

Giroux, H. A. (1992a). *Border crossings: Cultural workers and the politics of education.* New York: Routledge.

Giroux, H. A. (1992b, Spring). Post-colonial ruptures and democratic possibilities: Multiculturalism as anti-racist pedagogy. *Cultural Critique,* 5–39.

Giroux, H. A. (1993). *Living dangerously: Multiculturalism and the politics of difference.* New York: Peter Lang.

Giroux, H. A. (1996). *Fugitive cultures: Race, violence, and youth.* New York: Routledge.

Giroux, H. A. (1997). Rewriting the discourse of racial identity: Towards a pedagogy and politics of whiteness. *Harvard Educational Review, 67*(2), 285–320.

Goldberg, D. T. (1990). The social formation of racist discourse. In D. T. Goldberg (Ed.), *Anatomy of racism,* pp. 295–318. Minneapolis: University of Minnesota Press.

Goldberg, D. T. (1993a). Polluting the body politic: Racist discourse and the urban location. In M. Cross & M. Keith (Eds.), *Racism, the city and the state,* pp. 45–60. New York: Routledge.

Goldberg, D. T. (1993b). *Racist culture: Philosophy and the politics of meaning.* Cambridge, England: Blackwell.

Gooding-Williams, R. (Ed.). (1993). *Reading Rodney King, reading urban uprising.* New York: Routledge.

*Goodman, D. (1998). Lowering the shields: Reducing defensiveness in multicultural education. In R. Chávez Chávez & J. O'Donnell (Eds.), *Speaking the unpleasant: The politics of (non)engagement in the multicultural education terrain,* pp. 197–221. Albany: State University of New York Press.

Gould, S. J. (1996). *The mismeasure of man* (2nd Ed.). New York: W. W. Norton.

Gray, H. (1995). *Watching race.* Minneapolis: University of Minnesota Press.

Gresson, III, A. D. (1996). Postmodern America and the multicultural crisis: Reading Forrest Gump as the "call back to whiteness." *Taboo, 1,* 11–33.

Griffin, G. B. (1995). *Season of the witch: Borderlines, marginal notes.* Pasadena, CA: Trilogy Books.

Grundmann, J. (1994). Identity politics at face value: An interview with Scott McGehee and David Siegel. *Cineaste, 20*(3), 24–31.

Guiner, L. (1994). *The tyranny of the majority: Fundamental fairness in representative democracy*. New York: The Free Press.

Gussin Paley, V. (1979). *White teacher*. Cambridge, MA: Harvard University Press.

Hacker, A. (1992). *Two nations, Black and White, separate, hostile, unequal*. New York: Scribner's.

Haizlip, S. T. (1994). *The sweeter the juice*. New York: Simon & Schuster.

Haley, A. (1986). *The autobiography of Malcolm X as told to Alex Haley*. New York: Ballantine.

*Hall, S. (1990). Cultural identity and diaspora. In J. Rutherford (Ed.), *Identity, community, culture, difference*, pp. 222–237. London: Lawrence & Wishart.

Hall, S. (1991a). Ethnicity: Identity and difference. *Radical America, 13*(4), 9–20.

Hall, S. (1991b). Old and new identities, old, new ethnicities. In A. D. King (Ed.), *Culture, globalization and the world system*, pp. 41–68. Binghamton: State University of New York Press.

Hall, S. (1992). Race, culture, and communications: Looking backward and forward at cultural studies. *Rethinking Marxism, 5*(1), 13–27.

*Hall, S. (1995). Fantasy, identity, politics. In E. Carter, J. Donald, & J. Squires (Eds.), *Cultural remix*, pp. 67–82. London: Lawrence & Wishart.

Hall, S. (1996). New ethnicities. In D. Morley & K-H. Chen (Eds.), *Stuart Hall: Critical dialogues in cultural studies*, pp. 441–449. New York: Routledge.

Haney López, I. (1996). *White by law: The legal construction of race*. New York: New York University Press.

Hardiman, R. (1979). *White identity development*. Amherst, MA: New Perspectives.

Hardiman, R. (1982). White identity development: A process model for describing the racial consciousness of White Americans. *Dissertation Abstracts International, 432, 104A* (University Microfilms No. 82–10330).

Hardiman, R., & Jackson, B. W. (1992). Racial identity development: Understanding racial dynamics in college classrooms and on campus. In M. Adams (Ed.), *Promoting diversity in college classrooms: Innovative responses for the curriculum, faculty, and institutions*, pp. 213–223. San Francisco: Jossey-Bass.

Hardisty, J. (1996). My on-again, off-again romance with liberalism. *The Brown Papers*, 2(7), 12–22.

Haymes, S. N. (1995). *Race, culture, and the city*. Albany: State University of New York Press.

Helms, J. E. (1984). Toward a theoretical explanation of the effects of race on counseling: A Black and White model. *The Counseling Psychologist, 12*(4), 153–165.

Helms, J. E. (1990a). Toward a model of White racial identity development. In J. E. Helms (Ed.), *Black and White racial identity: Theory, research and practice*, pp. 49–66. Westport, CT: Greenwood.

Helms, J. E. (Ed.). (1990b). *Black and White racial identity: Theory, research and practice*. Westport, CT: Greenwood.

Helms, J. E. (1995). An update of Helms's White and People of Color racial identity models. In J. G. Ponterotto, J. M. Casas, L. A. Suzuki, & C. M. Alexander (Eds.), *Handbook of multicultural counseling*, pp. 142–167. Thousand Oaks, CA: Sage.

Herrnstein, R. J., & Murray, C. (1994). *The bell curve: Intelligence and class structure in American life*. New York: The Free Press.

Hidalgo, F., Chávez Chávez, R., & Ramage, J. (1996). Multicultural education: Landscape for reform in the 21st century. In J. Sikula & E. Guyton (Eds.), *Handbook of teacher education*, pp. 76–78. New York: MacMillan.

*Hispanic Educational Media Group, Saucelito, CA 94966. P(415) 332-2731, F(415) 331-2636.

hooks, b. (1989). *Talking back*. Boston: South End.

hooks, b. (1990). *Yearning*. Boston: South End.

hooks, b. (1992). *Black looks: Race and representation*. Boston: South End.

hooks, b. (1993). *Teaching to transgress: Education as the practice of freedom*. New York: Routledge.

hooks, b. (1995). *Killing rage*. New York: Henry Holt.

Howard, G. (1993). Whites in multicultural education: Rethinking our role. *Phi Delta Kappan, 75*(1), 36–41.

Hutchinson, E. O. (1994). *The assassination of the Black male image*. Los Angeles: Middle Passage.

Ignatiev, N. (1995). *How the Irish became White.* New York: Routledge.

Ignatiev, N. (1996). Editorial. In N. Ignatiev & J. Garvey (Eds.), *Race traitor*, pp. 2–3. New York: Routledge.

Ignatiev, N., & Garvey, J. (Eds.). (1996). *Race traitor.* New York: Routledge.

Jackson, III, B. W. (1976a). *The function of a Black identity development theory in achieving relevance in education for Black students.* Unpublished doctoral dissertation. University of Massachusetts, Amherst.

Jackson, III, B. W. (1976b). *Black identity development.* Amherst, MA: New Perspectives.

Jackson, B. W., & Hardiman, R. (1988). Oppression: Conceptual and developmental analysis. In M. Adams & L. Marchesani (Eds.), *Racial and cultural diversity, curricular content, and classroom dynamics: A manual for college teachers,* pp. 23–45. Amherst: University of Masachusetts Press.

*Jackson, D. (1995, November 1). Blacks vs. Whites: Through the looking glass. *The Boston Globe*, A12.

Jenkins, M. (1994). *Fear of the gansta'.* Unpublished doctoral dissertation. Northeastern University, Boston.

Jester, D. (1992). Roast beef and Reggae music: The passing of whiteness. *New Formations, 118,* 106–121.

Jhally, S. (1996). Dreamworlds 2: Desire/sex/power in music video [video]. Northampton, MA: Media Educational Foundation.

Johnson, M. (1995). Wanting to be Indian: When spiritual searching turns into cultural theft. *The Brown Papers, 1*(7), 1–17.

Kantrowitz, M. K. (1996). Jews in the U.S.: The rising costs of whiteness. In B. Thompson & S. Tyagi (Eds.), *Names we call home: Autobiography on racial identity,* pp. 22–43. New York: Routledge.

Karp, J. B. (1981). The emotional impact and a model for changing racist attitudes. In B. P. Bowser & R. G. Hunt (Eds.), *Impacts of racism on White Americans,* pp. 87–96. Beverly Hills, CA: Sage.

Katz, J. (1978). *White awareness: Handbook for antiracism training.* Norman: University of Oklahoma Press.

Keating, A. L. (1995). Interrogating "whiteness," (de)constructing "race." *College English, 57*(8), 907–922.

Kinchloe, J., Pinar, W. F., & Slattery, P. (1994). A last dying chord? Toward cultural and educational renewal in the South. *Curriculum Inquiry, 24*(2), 407–436.

Kohl, H. (1993). The myth of "Rosa Parks the tired." *Multicultural Education, 1*(2), 6–10.

Kovel, J. (1984). *White racism: A psychohistory.* New York: Columbia University Press.

Kozol, J. (1991). *Savage inequalities: Children in America's schools.* New York: Crown.

Kuhn, A., & Wolpe, A. M. (1978). *Feminism and materialism: Women and modes of production.* London: Routledge & Kegan Paul.

Kunjufu, J. (1995). *Countering the conspiracy to destroy Black boys (Vol. 1).* Chicago: African American Images.

LaClau, E., & Mouffe, C. (1990). *Hegemony & socialist strategy: Towards a radical democratic politics.* London: Verso.

Laclau, E. (1992). Universalism, particularism, and the question of identity, *October, 61*(2), 83–90.

Laing, R. D., & Cooper, D. G. (1971). *Reason and violence: A decade of Sartre's philosophy 1950–1960.* New York: Random House.

Lam, A., & Pruyn, M. (1998). *Linguistic affirmative action.* Unpublished manuscript. New Mexico State University, Las Cruces.

Lazarus, E. (1991). *Black hills White justice: The Sioux Nation versus the United States 1775 to the present.* New York: Harper Collins.

Lee, S. (1996). *Unraveling the "model minority" stereotype: Listening to Asian American youth.* New York: Teachers College Press.

Lipsitz, G. (1995). The possessive investment in whiteness: Racialized social democracy and the "White" problem in American studies. *American Quarterly, 47*(3), 369–387.

Lipsitz, G. (1996). "It's all wrong, but it's all right": Creative misunderstandings in intercultural communication. In A. Gordon & C. Newfield (Eds.), *Mapping multiculturalism,* pp. 403–412. Minneapolis: University of Minnesota Press.

Loewen, J. W. (1995). *Lies my teacher told me: Everything your American history textbook got wrong.* New York: The New Press.

Loiacano, D. K. (1989). Gay identity issues among Black Americans: Racism, homophobia and the need for validation. *Journal of Counseling and Development*, 68(5), 21–25.

Lorde, A. (1984). *Sister outsider*. New York: Crossing.

Loveday, L. (1982). *The sociolinguistics of learning and using a non-native language*. Oxford: Pergamon.

Macedo, D. (1994). *Literacies of power*. Boulder: Westview.

Macedo, D., & Bartolomé, L. (in press). Dancing with bigotry: The poisoning of racial and ethnic identities. In E. Torres Trueba & Y. Zou (Eds.), *Ethnic identity and power*, pp. 112–126. Albany: State University of New York Press.

Mandela, N. (1990). *Nelson Mandela: The struggle is my life*. New York: Pathfinder.

Manning, M. L. (1995). Understanding culturally diverse parents and families. *Equity & Excellence in Education, 28*(1), 52–57.

Marquez, P. (1996). *A Navajo identity development model*. Unpublished manuscript. New Mexico State University, Las Cruces.

Marshall, C. (1991). Palos, piedras, y estereotipos/Sticks, stones, and stereotypes [video]. Amherst, MA: Equity Institute.

Marx, K. (1904). *A contribution to the critique of political economy*. Chicago: Charles H. Kerr.

Mathison, C., & Young, R. (1995). Constructivism and multicultural education. *Multicultural Education, 2*, 7–10.

McCall, A. L. (1995). We were cheated! Students' responses to a multicultural, social reconstructionist teacher education course. *Equity & Excellence in Education, 28*(1), 15–24.

McCarthy, C., & Critchlow, W. (Eds.). (1993). *Race identity and representation in education*. New York: Routledge.

McLean Donaldson, K. B. (1996). *Through students' eyes: Combatting racism in United States schools*. Westport, CT: Praeger.

McCormick, J., & Begley, S. (1996, December 9). How to raise a Tiger. *Sports Illustrated*, 52–59.

McGowan, J. (1991). *Postmodernism and its critics.* Ithaca, NY: Cornell University Press.

McIntosh, P. (1983). *Interactive phases of curricular development.* Wellesley, MA: Wellesley Center for Research on Women.

McIntosh, P. (1989). White privilege: Unpacking the invisible knapsack. *Peace and Freedom, 4,* 10–12.

McIntosh, P. (1992). White privilege and male privilege: A personal account of coming to see correspondences through work in women's studies. In P. H. Collins & M. Andersen (Eds.), *Race, class and gender: An anthology,* pp. 67–81. Belmont, CA: Wadsworth.

McLaren, P. (1995). *Critical pedagogy and predatory culture.* New York: Routledge.

Mclaren, P. (1997). *Revolutionary multiculturalism: Pedagogies of dissent for the new millennium.* Boulder: Westview.

Media Educational Foundation (1996). The myth of the liberal media: The propaganda model of news [video]. Northhampton, MA: Media Educational Foundation.

Miller, J. G. (1996). *Search and destroy: African-American males in the criminal justice system.* New York: Cambridge University Press.

Monthly Review Press, 122 West 27th Street, New York, NY 10001. F(212) 727-3676. E-Mail: mreview@igc.apc.org.

Moraga, C., & Anzaldúa, G. (1981). *This bridge called my back: Writings by radical Women of Color.* Watertown, MA: Persephone.

Morales, M. (1996). *Bilingual education: A dialogue with the Bakhtin Circle.* Albany: State University of New York Press.

Morrison, T. (1992). *Playing in the dark: Whiteness in the literary imagination.* Cambridge, MA: Harvard University Press.

Mura, D. (1991). *Turning Japanese: Memoirs of a Sansei.* New York: Atlantic Monthly.

Mun Wah, L. (1994). The color of fear [video]. Oakland, CA: Stir-Fry Productions.

Nakayama, T. K., & Krizek, R. L. (1995). Whiteness: A strategic rhetoric. *Quarterly Journal of Speech, 81,* 291–309.

Neufeldt, V., & Guralnik, D. B. (1997). *Webster's new world college dictionary.* Cleveland: MacMillan.

Nicholson, L. J. (1990). *Feminism/postmodernism: Thinking gender.* New York: Routledge.

Nieto, S. (1996). *Affirming diversity: The sociopolitical context of multicultural education.* White Plains, NY: Longman.

Nieto, S. (1998). From claiming hegemony to sharing space: Creating community in multicultural courses. In R. Chávez Chávez & J. O'Donnell (Eds.), *Speaking the unpleasant: The politics of resistance in the multicultural education terrain,* pp. 111–134. New York: State University of New York Press.

Nike (1995a). If you let me play sports. Commercial # 95–12807 30. New York: Nike.

Nike (1995b). Ric Muñoz. Commercial # 95–02058 30. New York: Nike.

Novick, M. (1995). *White lies, White power.* Monroe, ME: Common Courage.

Oakes, J. (1985). *Keeping track: How schools structure inequality.* New Haven: Yale University Press.

O'Brien, C. C. (1996, October). Thomas Jefferson: Radical and racist. *The Atlantic Monthly,* 53–74.

*O'Donnell, J. (1995). Toward an anti-racist pedagogy: A theoretical instructional paradigm. In A. Nava (Ed.), *Educating Americans in a multiethnic society,* pp. 34–48. New York: McGraw-Hill.

Ogbu, J. (1986). Black students' school success: Coping with the "burden of 'acting White.'" *The Urban Review, 18*(3), 176–206.

Omi, M., & Winant, H. (1994). *Racial formations in the United States from the 1960s to 1990s.* New York: Routledge.

Perea, J. F. (1995). Los olvidados: On the making of unvisible people. *New York University Law Review, 70*(4), 965–991.

Pfeil, F. (1995). *White guys: Studies in postmodern domination and difference.* London: Verso.

Pietri, P. (1989). *The Puerto Rican obituary.* New York: Monthly Review.

Pinar, W. F. (1997). Notes on understanding curriculum as a racial text. In C. McCarthy & W. Crichlow (Eds.), *Race, identity and representation in* education, pp. 134–147. New York: Routledge.

Powell, R. (1996). Confronting white hegemony. *Multicultural Education, 4*, 12–15.

Public Broadcasting System. (1992). Eyes on the prize [video]. New York: Time Life.

Public Broadcasting System. (1994). ¡Chicano! [video]. Saucelito, CA: Hispanic Educational Media Group.

Rattansi, A. (1994). "Western" racisms, ethnicities and identities in a "postmodern" frame. In A. Rattansi & S. Westwood (Eds.), *Racism, modernity and identity on the western front*, pp. 403–412. Cambridge, England: Polity.

Rethinking Schools, 1001 East Keefe Avenue, Milwaukee, WI 53212. P(414) 964-9646, F(414) 964-7220. www.rethinkingschools.org.

Rethinking Schools. (1992). *Rethinking Columbus*. Milwaukee, WI: Rethinking Schools.

Rich, A. (1979). "Disloyal to civilization": Feminism, racism, gynephobia. In A. Rich (Ed.), *On lies, secrets and silences*, pp. 56–69. New York: Norton.

Reilly, R. (1996, October 26). Top cat. *Sports Illustrated*, 46–50.

Roediger, D. (1991). *The wages of whiteness*. London: Verso.

Roediger, D. (1994). *Towards the abolition of whiteness* London: Verso.

Rorty, R. (1989). *Contingency, irony, and solidarity*. New York: Cambridge University Press.

Rosaldo, R. (1993). *Culture & truth*. Boston: Beacon Press.

Rose, W. (1992). The great pretenders: Further reflections on Whiteshamanism. In M. A. Jaimes (Ed.), *The state of Native America: Genocide, colonization, and resistance*, pp. 117–138. Boston: South End.

Rosenberg, P. M. (1997). Underground discourses: Exploring whiteness in teacher education. In M. Fine, L. Weis, L. C. Powell, & L. M. Wong (Eds.), *Off white: Readings on race, power, and society*, pp. 79–89. New York: Routledge.

*Rowe, W., Bennett, S. K., & Atkinson, D. R. (1994). White racial identity models: A critique and alternative proposal. *The Counseling Psychologist, 22*(1), 129–146.

Said, Edward. (1985). *Orientalism*. London: Penguin.

San Juan Jr., E. (1991). The culture of ethnicity and the fetish of pluralism: A counterhegemonic critique. *Cultural Critique, 21*, 221–236.

Sartre, J. P. (1976). *Critique of dialectical reason research I: Theory of practical ensembles*. London: New Left Books.

Saxton, A. (1991). *The rise and fall of the White republic*. London: Verso.

*Scheurich, J. J. (1993a). Toward a White discourse on White racism. *Educational Researcher, 22*(8), 5–15.

*Scheurich, J. J. (1993b). A difficult, confusing, painful problem that requires many voices, many perspectives. *Educational Researcher, 22*(8), 15–16.

Schwartz, B. (Ed.). (1993). *Educating for civic responsibility in a multicultural world*. Swarthmore, PA: Swarthmore College Press.

*Segrest, M. (1994a). *My mama's dead squirrel: Lesbian essays on southern culture*. Ithaca, NY: Firebrand Books.

*Segrest, M. (1994b). *Memoir of a race traitor*. Boston: South End.

Seldon, H. (1992). The "new" racism???? *Convictions about racism in the United States of America*. Boston: Community Change.

Shepard, T., & Magnaye, M. (1998). Camp Lavender Hill [video]. San Francisco: Camp Lavender Hill Documentary Project.

Shohat, E., & Stam, R. (1994). *Unthinking eurocentrism*. New York: Routledge.

Shor, I. (1992). *Empowering education: Critical teaching for social change*. Chicago: University of Chicago Press.

Sleeter, C. E., & Grant, C. A. (1991). Race, class, gender and disability in current textbooks. In M. W. Apple & L. K. Christian-Smith. *The politics of the textbook*, pp. 79–91. New York: Routledge & Chapman Hall.

*Sleeter, C. E. (1993). Advancing a White discourse: A response to Scheurich. *Educational Researcher, 22*(8), 13–15.

Sleeter, C. E. (1996). *Multicultural education as social activism*. Albany: State University of New York Press.

Smart, B. (1992). *Postmodern controversies*. New York: Routledge.

Smith, G. (1991). *Culture*. Unpublished manuscript. Quinsigamond Community College, Worcester, Massachusetts.

Snead, J. (1994). *White screens, Black images* New York: Routledge.

Southern Poverty Law Center (1995). The shadow of hate: A history of intolerance in America [video]. Montgomery, AL: Teaching Tolerance, Southern Poverty Law Center.

Spring, J. (1997). *Deculturalization and the struggle for equality: A brief history of the education of dominated cultures in the United States* (2nd Ed.). New York: McGraw-Hill.

*Stalvey, L. (1988). *The education of a WASP*. Madison: University of Wisconsin Press.

Stephancic, J., & Delgado, R. (1996). *No mercy: How conservative think tanks and foundations changed America's social agenda*. Philadelphia: Temple University Press.

Stowe, D. W. (1996). Uncolored people: The rise of whiteness studies. *Lingua Franca, 6*(6), 68–77.

Sue, D. W., & Sue, D. (1990). *Counseling the culturally different: Theory and practice*. New York: John Wiley.

Szasz, T. (1970). *The manufacture of madness: A comparative study of the inquisition and the mental health movement*. New York: Dell.

Takaki, R. (1993). *A different mirror: A multicultural history of America*. Boston: Little, Brown & Company.

Tatum, B. D. (1987). *Assimilation blues: Black families in a White community*. Northamption, MA: Hazel-Maxwell.

Tatum, B. D. (1992). Talking about race, learning about racism: The application of racial identity development theory in the classroom. *Harvard Educational Review, 62*(1), 1–24.

Tatum, B. D. (1994). Teaching White students about racism: The search for White allies and the restoration of hope. *Teachers College Record, 95*(4), 462–76.

Tatum, B. D. (1997). *Why are all the Black kids sitting together in the cafeteria? and other conversations about race.* New York: Basic Books.

Teaching Tolerance, Southern Poverty Law Center, 400 Washinton Avenue, Montgomery, AL 36104. Editorial F(334) 264-3121, Order Department F(334) 264-7310. www.splcenter.org.

Terkel, S. (1992). *Race: How Blacks and Whites think and feel about the American obsession.* New York: The New Press.

Terry, R. (1975). *For Whites only.* Grand Rapids, WI: William B. Erdmans.

Terry, R. (1981). The negative impact of White values. In B. P. Bowser & R. G. Hunt (Eds.), *Impacts of racism on White Americans,* pp. 111–134. Beverly Hills: Sage.

Thomas, A., & Sillen, S. (1972). *Racism and psychiatry.* New York: Brunner/Mazel.

Thompson, B. (1996). Time traveling and border crossing: Reflections on White identity. In B. Thompson & S. Tyagi (Eds.), *Names we call home: Autobiography on racial identity,* pp. 142–161. Minneapolis: University of Minnesota Press.

Thompson, B. & Tyagi, S. (1993). The politics of inclusion: Reskilling the academy. In S. Tyagi & B. Thompson (Eds.), *Beyond a dream deferred: Multicultural education and the politics of excellence,* pp. 23–43. Minneapolis: University of Minnesota Press.

*Thompson, B., & White Women Challenging Racism. (1997). Home/work: Antiracism activism and the meaning of whiteness. In M. Fine, L. Weis, L. C. Powell, & L. M. Wong (Eds.), *Off white: Readings on race, power, and society,* pp. 354–366. New York: Routledge.

Thompson, L. (1996). *Whitefolks: Seeing America through Black eyes.* Self-Published, Lowell Thompson, 1507 E. 53rd Street, Unit 132, Chicago, IL, 60615.

Time Table of African American History (1997). [On-line]. Available: http://www.msstate.edu/listarchives/afrigeneas/199707/msg00582.html.

Van Sertima, I. (1976). *They came before Columbus.* New York: Random House.

Van Sertima, I. (Ed.). (1992). *African presence in early America.* New Brunwisk, NJ: Transaction.

Walsh, C. (1991). *Pedagogy and the struggle for voice: Issues of language, power, and schooling for Puerto Ricans.* New York: Bergin & Garvey.

Ware, V. (1992). *Beyond the pale: White women, racism, and history.* London: Verso.

Warner, M. (1993). *Fear of a Queer planet: Queer politics and social theory.* Minneapolis: University of Minnesota Press.

Webster, Y. (1992). *The racialization of America.* New York: St. Martin's.

Weinstein, G., & Obear, K. (1992). Bias issues in the Classroom: Encounters with the teaching self. In M. Adams (Ed.), *Promoting diversity in college classrooms: Innovative responses for the curriculum, faculty, and institutions,* pp. 52–67. San Francisco: Jossey-Bass.

Wellesley Center for Research on Women, Wellesley College, 106 Central Street, Wellesley, MA 02182. P(617) 283-2500, F(617) 283-2504. www.wellesley.edu/ WCW/crwsub.html.

Wellman, D. (1993). *Portraits of White racism* (2nd Ed.). New York: Cambridge University Press.

Wellman, D. (1996). Red and Black in America. In B. Thompson & S. Tyagi (Eds.), *Names we call home: Autobiography on racial identity,* pp. 291–215. New York: Routledge.

Welsing, F. C. (1970). *The Cress theory of color, confrontation, and racism (white supremacy).* Washington, DC: C-R Publishers.

Wiley, W. (1991, December 16). Students raise concerns in fight against weapons. *Worcester Transcript & Telegram,* A3.

*Williams, P. J. (1991). *The alchemy of race and rights: Diary of a law professor.* Cambridge, MA: Harvard University Press.

Williams, R. (1970). *American society.* New York: Knopf.

*Wilson, W. J. (1980). *The declining significance of race.* Chicago: University of Chicago Press.

Women's Health Clinic (1986). *Female distance runners and the Pope.* Gainesville, FL: Women's Health Clinic.

Worcester Historical Museum, 30 Elm Street, Worcester, MA 01609 P(508) 753-8278.

*Women of the South Asian Diaspora (1993). *Our feet walk the sky.* San Francisco: Aunt Lute.

*Yarbro-Bejarano, Y. (1994). Gloria Anzaldua's borderlands/la frontera: Cultural studies, "difference," and the non-unitary subject. *Cultural Critique, 3*, 5–28.

Young, L. (1990). A nasty piece of work: A psychoanalytic study of sexual and racial difference in "Mona Lisa." In J. Rutherford (Ed.), *Identity: Community, culture, difference*, pp. 188–206. London: Lawrence & Wishart.

Young, R. (1990). *White mythologies: Writing history and the west.* New York: Routledge.

Young, V. (1979). *Towards an increased understanding of whiteness in relation to White racism.* Unpublished manuscript. University of Massachusetts, Amherst.

*Young, W. (1969). *Beyond racism.* New York: McGraw-Hill.

*Yudice, G. (1995). Neither impugning nor disavowing whiteness does a viable politics make: The limits of identity politics. In C. Newfield & R. Strickland (Eds.), *After political correctness*, pp. 255–281. Boulder: Westview.

Zinn, Howard. (1970). *The politics of history.* Boston: Beacon Press.

Zinn, H. (1980). *A people's history of the United States.* New York: Harper & Row.

NOTES

[1]Additional resources (i.e., sources not cited in the text of this guide) are preceded by an asterisk.

About the Author

Christine Clark is an Associate Professor of Educational Studies and the Coordinator of the Urban Educational Leadership Doctoral Program at the University of Cinncinnati. Her research explores the development of multicultural education to "disarm" violence in schools and communities; the trend in civil law toward becoming more race neutral and the trend in criminal law toward becoming more race conscious and the resulting escalation of institutionalized racism; and, racial identity development theory, in particular, the emergence of anti-racist consciousness in Whites.